REMEMBER
Me

To Katie ~
Sharing my "story" with you about our special years in St Louis.

Janale
(MCC Sarasota)

REMEMBER *Me*

A Memoir of Children and Teens Combating Cancer

Janalee Tomaseski-Heinemann, MSW

Adam's Angels Publishing, LLC
Sarasota, FL

© 2019 Janalee Tomaseski-Heinemann

All rights reserved. No part of this publication may be reproduced, stored in a retrieval system, or transmitted in any form or by any means electronic, mechanical, photocopying, recording or otherwise, without the prior written permission of the publisher. This book may not be copied or reprinted for commercial gain or profit. The use of short quotations or occasional page copying for personal or group study is permitted and encouraged. Permission will be granted upon request.

Published by
Adam's Angels Publishing, LLC
Sarasota, FL

Publisher's Cataloging-in-Publication Data
Tomaseski-Heinemann, Janalee.

   Remember me : a memoir of children and teens combating cancer / Janalee Tomaseski-Heinemann. – Sarasota, FL : Adam's Angels Pub., LLC, 2019.

   p. ; cm.

   ISBN13: 978-0-9600853-0-9

   1. Cancer in children—Psychological aspects. 2. Medical social work—Missouri—St. Louis. I. Title.

RC281.C4 T66 2019
618.92994—dc23   2019930025

Project Coordination by Jenkins Group Inc.
www.bookpublishing.com

Front cover photo: Kris Selberg, M.D., teen cancer survior (photograph by Dan Lehr)
Cover and interior design by Yvonne Fetig Roehler

Printed in the United States of America
23 22 21 20 19 • 5 4 3 2 1

Adam Romagnoli

This book is dedicated to our bright, handsome, charming grandson, Adam Romagnoli, who like many of the children and teens in this book, died much too young in an accident at age eighteen.

It is also dedicated to his mother, our daughter, Tracy White, who had the courage to go on living and to find new purpose and joy after dedicating her life to Adam.

Before Cancer

*M*any years before I worked with children with cancer, I volunteered for a family whose three sons had Duchenne's muscular dystrophy. I was closest to the oldest son, twenty-one-year-old Bill Riley, and was with him during his final days. Although he slowly lost the use of all the muscles in his body, Bill's mind was fine until the end. When he began losing the muscles that controlled his voice and knew he would soon be unable to speak, I held his hand and leaned my ear close to his mouth so I could hear his whispers. One of the last things Bill said to me was, *"Don't forget my name."*

I have not forgotten you, Bill. I have always felt I owe it to all the beautiful children and teens I worked with who had cancer not to forget their names or stories either.

Bill Riley

February 10, 1953–January 11, 1975

Contents

Foreword xi
Introduction xiii
1   I Walked with Angels 1
2   And Then There Were Nine 33
3   Teen Trip to Florida 69
4   Tips and Insights from the Teens 77
5   Beyond the Child with Cancer 83
6   It's Not Over When It's Over 91
7   Poignant Final Days 97
8   Lessons from a Bereaved Mom 109
9   Personal Reflections 119
10 Cancer Hits Home 127
    Epilogue 149
    Acknowledgments 151
    About the Author 155

Foreword

As she retires from a distinguished two-decade career with the Prader-Willi Syndrome Association, Janalee Tomaseski-Heinemann has returned to fulfill a promise she made many years ago to children who were dying of cancer in St. Louis Children's Hospital where she was an oncology social worker. She promised she would not forget them, and she hasn't. In this book, she tells their stories with loving honesty and, in so doing, allows us to share the intense way their lives and deaths became intertwined with hers.

Janalee was my student, then a colleague in the early days of my study of bereaved parents. During her years at the hospital, she and I had many conversations. I remember being awestruck by her work and the effect she had on the parents I knew. I have often told the story of how she organized a trip to Florida for teenagers with cancer and a support team of nurses, physicians, and parents.

Cancer does not respect any of the boundaries we would like to draw. Janalee shares her feelings, thoughts, and what she did as a mother when her own child was diagnosed with cancer. This was not unlike those she knew at the hospital, though her child was a middle-aged man when he was diagnosed.

When we are in the presence of death and dying children, we know what is important and what is not. Janalee's book is about the children and teenagers living in that presence and also about their parents. Hers is far more than a sad book because the children have left a legacy for us to learn from. Janalee does us the favor of transmitting that profound legacy to us.

— DENNIS KLASS, PH.D.. author of *The Spiritual Lives of Bereaved Parents* and co-editor of *Dead but Not Lost: Grief Narratives in Religious Traditions*.

Introduction

Over a ten-year period from 1985–1995, I worked with 128 children who died of cancer and many others who lived. During that time at St. Louis Children's Hospital (SLCH), my heart and soul were consumed and intertwined with their lives. At that time, I did not use my full name, Janalee Tomaseski-Heinemann. I was known as Jan Tomaseski, the pediatric oncology social worker who always had a clipboard and pen on a chain around her neck.

When you read this book, please remember that, in many ways, treatment was even more difficult twenty-three years ago than it is today. We did not have good anti-nausea drugs, drugs to relieve the pain of spinal taps and bone marrow aspirates, drugs to boost the immune system, or many other helpful drugs. Although it has been many years since I lived and breathed childhood cancer, I kept notes knowing that someday I would share them. Some stories are too beautiful, too profound, too sad, too inspiring, and too spiritual *not* to be told.

Besides paying tribute to the children and families who lived these stories, I hope to give some insight into what is helpful to know and understand in order to support families whose children are stricken with cancer. How often have we felt totally helpless when trying to support someone going through a medical and emotional crisis? Sometimes we say the wrong thing when we hoped to be profound and comforting. Worse yet is when we avoid the person in crisis or grieving because we don't know what to say. This discomfort is also a problem for people in the medical field. They are taught to care for the body, but seldom are they taught to care for the spirit and soul.

Sooner or later, cancer impacts everyone. Professionally, it consumed my life for the ten years I worked at SLCH. Years later, I was diagnosed with breast cancer, then my husband with prostate cancer. I wrote one of the chapters on the teens in this book twenty-three years ago before setting the project aside. Ironically, shortly after I picked it up again, our grown up and wonderful son, Tad, was diagnosed with a very difficult head and neck cancer. When I reread that chapter, I saw the words, "...never knowing if and when the elusive killer would shatter their lives again." This time it is our family trying to avoid the elusive killer.

I don't want to give the impression that this book is all about sadness and tragedy. It is also about the celebration of the indomitable spirit of the child, the wonderful honesty and bond of teenagers being treated for cancer, and my profound sense that there must be something after this life.

Dying children don't lie. They are often given the gift of a vision of what is waiting for them beyond the walls of the hospital and their parents' arms. It is my privilege to share these beautiful angels and their visions with you.

Fortunately, I kept all my personal notes from the years I worked at St. Louis Children's Hospital, so the stories and words are accurate. In my longer tributes to the children and teens, I use their full names with their family's permission to tell their stories. Where I have not been able to track down the families, I tell shorter stories and just use first names and ages. If any of these children or families read this book, I hope they will reconnect with me because each and every one of their children remains deep in my heart. Their spirits helped form who I am today.

Introduction

Doris, the mother of Jason Struble, told me she was glad I was writing this book because Jason's greatest fear was that he would not be remembered. This fear was common in the teens who knew they were dying and also common in their parents. We felt this fear too. When our grandson Adam was killed in an accident, we included the following poem in his memorial card:

> ### I Speak Your Name
>
> *I had realized that after a while no one would say the name of the child I lost.*
>
> *It is as though by not saying his name, they can somehow escape the pain.*
>
> *But, I need to hear his name. I want to hear his name out loud.*
>
> *It means so much to me to hear him validated this way.*
>
> *His life was important, and his death was important.*
>
> *By speaking the names of our dead, we bring life to our memories.*
>
> *Yes, even when it's painful, it is welcomed.*
>
> *I don't mind crying for him.*
>
> *It reminds me that I'm still human enough to cry.*
>
> ~ Author Unknown

I wrote this book to speak their names, to tell their stories, and to immortalize the beautiful spirits of those children and teenagers stricken with cancer.

I also wrote this book to honor their families and to help others understand how to be supportive. As adeptly stated by a Crosier priest: "We can't prevent people from suffering, but we can see to it that people don't suffer for the wrong reasons."

I Walked with Angels

*L*iving, loving, laughing, crying, and dying were all part of the roller coaster ride I took while working as a social worker at the pediatric hematology/oncology unit at St. Louis Children's Hospital. I was fortunate to be doing medical social work in an era where I could be creative in creating programs and where we all shared the belief that "rules are meant to be smiled at." With hospice and pediatric oncology, when you're dealing with a person who is dying, you learn to be humane first and a "rule keeper" second.

The following stories remember just a few of the amazing children I worked with during my ten years at SLCH. Upon learning that I was a pediatric social worker, people typically told me, "Oh, I could *never* work with children who had cancer; it would just be too sad!" These individuals did not appreciate what a gift it was to have my life touched by angels. Once you read their stories, you will understand why I felt so privileged to share their lives and why, today, I can still feel their spirits.

Kalilah Johnson: 1977–1990

"I couldn't die right then because he would have felt sooo guilty!"

Ten-year-old Kalilah was diagnosed with rhabdomyosarcoma in the muscle in her left leg in October of 1987. Her cancer was very aggressive, and she was not in treatment for long before it became apparent that she was fighting a losing battle. An unusually spiritual girl, Kalilah read the Bible every day. When her cancer progressed, she had her mother tape her reading it out loud so that she could hear the Bible in her own words once she became too weak to read. Kalilah had a smile that lit up the room, and when she lost her curly black hair, she looked just as beautiful.

Shortly before Kalilah's death, when I was sitting next to her hospital bed, she told me she'd never been to St. Louis's famous Gateway Arch and had always wanted to go. Knowing her time was very limited, I got her mother, Neithy's, permission and called Al to request his help.

Both Al and I were frantically busy that day, so by the time we arrived and got Kalilah out of the car, the arch was about to close. We ran across the park grounds, pushing Kalilah in a wheelchair and making jokes about practicing for a marathon. As she laughed, I silently prayed we'd make it before the 6:00 p.m. closing.

When we arrived, the ticket booth woman was putting up the closed sign. My heart sank. I told Al to wait with Kalilah by the indoor pond while I privately pleaded our case. When I explained that next week and possibly tomorrow would not be an option for Kalilah, the ticket booth woman talked to the man who ran the trams to the top of the arch, and they agreed to add an extra ride.

As Al carried Khalili into the tram, I thought with gratitude how special Al was and how lucky I was to encounter employees who understood the need for an exception to every rule.

Two nights before she died, not long after visiting the arch, Al and I spent the evening with Kalilah and her family at her home. At that point, the tumor was closing off most of her esophagus, making eating almost impossible. She was only able to talk in whispers, but her beautiful spirit and sense of humor were intact. She told us about the trip she and her parents had taken to Chicago a few days earlier so she could see her extended family before she died. At one point, they had attempted to feed her in the car, but she began to choke. Her dad had pulled over to the side of the interstate and pulled her limp body out of the car, pleading, "You can't die! You can't die! Please God, don't let her die like this!"

Kalilah told me that her dad shook her body and did the Heimlich maneuver on her until her limp body suddenly began wiggling from her feet all the way to her fingertips. "Like magic," she said, she came back to life.

Kalilah looked at me with her big eyes, smiled her beautiful smile, and whispered, "I couldn't die right then because he would have felt sooo guilty!"

It was a special night. Her uncle Alif, an attorney, made spaghetti for everyone. This was Kalilah's favorite dish, and she begged me to feed her some. With her mother's permission, I smashed the spaghetti and sauce into a pureed substance, fed her tiny spoonfuls, and prayed it would go down. It did, and she whispered "Thank you" several times. Later, we all stood around Kalilah's bed in the living room, held hands, prayed for her, and sang. This was a family and a night blessed by the Lord.

The next night, I was called to the hospital at 2:00 a.m. When I arrived, Kalilah was choking and gasping for breath, her eyes wide in terror. I prayed, "Please, Lord, don't let her die like this! Don't let this be her family's last memories of her."

Despite oxygen, there had been no relief from her choking for fifteen hours. The doctor came in to say he thought her death would come at any moment. Moments later, Kalilah sat straight up in bed, stopped gasping, talked clearly, and even smiled and kidded with us.

Her mom asked if she was in pain, and Kalilah told her no, that she was in a river of water. She said she could see her mom and dad far away and kept reaching for them. At first she couldn't get to them, she said, but eventually she made it back. She then told everyone she loved them, lay back in bed, and died with a peaceful smile on her face.

I have given up trying to find fairness in this world, and at times I have struggled with my faith and the concept of a heaven, but what I learned about Kalilah when she was six years old gives me a lot to think about. Diagnosed with diabetes at age six, years before her diagnosis of rhabdomyosarcoma, Kalilah was eight when she told her family she'd had a visit from the Lord. He'd told her she would be healed when she was twelve and that she would not be alone.

On January 5, 1990, in her hospital bed, twelve-year-old Kalilah was "healed" of her pain and suffering. The next day, her grandmother Edna died and the family held a double funeral for them.

Kalilah was not alone.

Left to right: Janalee, Mindy Ostoff, and Al

Mindy Ostoff: 1976–1988

"After my surgery, I won't be able to see Christmas again, but now I get to!"

By the time Mindy was eleven years old, she had lost both of her eyes but not her spirit. The youngest of eight children, Mindy was the baby of the family and loved by all. First diagnosed at age two with tumors in both eyes due to retinoblastoma, she'd had her right eye removed. She had some vision impairment in her left eye due to scarring from the tumor and from radiation therapy, but she could see. Despite treatment including chemotherapy, the cancer resurfaced in her left temple in 1984 when she was seven. This was when I first met Mindy and her mother, Shirley, with whom I'm in regular contact to this day.

Mindy's new cancer was considered a second malignancy, probably an undifferentiated sarcoma, possibly due to the radiation she'd had when she was younger.

Mindy was a very wise little girl. I was sitting with her while her parents were in the conference room with the doctor getting the bad news and details of treatment when Mindy stated, "I should be in there too because I am the one who has to go through it!"

In 1986, cancer was found in the lymph nodes in Mindy's neck. In June of that year, cancer was discovered in the maxillary sinus behind her left cheekbone. Initial attempts to control the cancer with chemotherapy were unsuccessful, and Mindy made the decision on her own to remove her other eye in an attempt to save her life.

In our desire to give Mindy some special memories before the surgery that would leave her blind, we held an early surprise Christmas party in November for her in the auditorium at the hospital. Santa came and gave her many presents. Sweet Mindy giggled and said with a big smile, "After my surgery, I won't be able to see Christmas again, but now I get to!" Fortunately, what she didn't see were the tears in all our eyes and those of the reporter.

Mindy loved Barbies and arranged everything at home so that she would be able to find her dolls and toys after she lost her vision. She also insisted on going back to school despite chemotherapy and being blind. I'll never forget that a month before Mindy died, at the invitation of her mother, we attended a United Church of Christ dinner in Augusta, Missouri. Although Mindy was blind and in pain, she filled cups with ice, wrapped silverware, and entertained guests by playing songs on her electronic organ, smiling all the while.

Just two and a half weeks before she died, we took Mindy on a trip sponsored by Dream Factory, a non-profit dedicated to providing wish trips, to Silver Dollar City with other children from St. Louis Children's Hospital. Mindy's mom came along, and bless

Shirley's brave heart, she didn't once tell Mindy she couldn't do something. Each night, the nurse, Barb Carr, and I held our breath, praying Mindy would still be alive in the morning. Although she was too weak to walk and so full of cancer that she could hardly breathe, Mindy insisted on going on the Thunder River water ride. Much to the dismay of the staff, Al carried her to the ride, and we wrapped her up to keep her as dry as possible. We snuggled with her in the ride to cushion any bumps as we all went careening down and around the artificial river with Mindy screaming with glee. It might sound crazy, but how do you say no to a little girl who is going to die no matter what you do within a matter of days or weeks?

Instead of returning on the early bus like many of the kids, Mindy stayed as long as possible and even went to some of the night shows. She eked every bit of joy out of this trip that she possibly could.

Shirley and Mindy talked openly about dying. Shirley said, "She didn't want to leave us, but she didn't have any choice." During the last months, they talked a lot about what heaven would be like. Mindy knew it would be good, but she didn't know if she was ready to go. She loved life and loved her family, and they all loved her dearly. I'm grateful that Mindy died peacefully, surrounded by her family.

After she died, her sister Mary wrote, "Why couldn't God let Mindy have a normal life like everyone else? Why couldn't God let Mindy grow up to be an adult? Why? Why? Why?" As for me, I'd long ago stopped searching for an answer to "Why." It was the only way I could do what I did for so many years.

Darren Sanders: 1981–1991

"He might have been a frail little boy on the outside, but he was tall and bright and strong and full of grace on the inside."

Darren was diagnosed with leukemia at age five. He had three years of treatment but relapsed after being off treatment for eighteen months. He was from a close-knit family that included four younger siblings, so when the family learned a bone marrow transplant was his best hope, family and friends alike rallied.

What I remember the most about Darren was his incredible maturity for a ten-year-old boy. He once said to me, "I think it's really silly those doctors have meetings right outside my room." Due to the large glass windows facing the hallway in each room, you could see everything. "You would think they would go meet in private," he added.

Darren had an amazing faith in God. He said, "With God as my guide, I am going to get better sooner or later." Yet this kind and gentle soul knew that "getting better" might not happen on this Earth.

One elderly friend recalled visiting Darren in the transplant unit a few days before he died, where in spite of all the agonizing treatment and side effects, he never once complained. After spending the night with him, as this friend was preparing to leave, Darren thanked him for coming and said, "Will you tell me a prayer?" After they held hands and prayed, Darren smiled and weakly waved.

The friend said, "He touched me deep in my soul by being himself. Never have I seen greater courage. This young man was a minister of God to me. He might have been a frail little boy on the outside, but he was tall and bright and strong and full of grace on the inside."

I had the privilege of speaking at Darren's funeral. I talked about how some of the best children seem to suffer the most. I said that although I often see pain and sorrow, I also see goodness and compassion through the medical staff and families, and I see a glimpse of heaven because dying children do not lie.

I concluded, "People often lament and ask for proof that God exists. What better confirmation is there that God and goodness exist than in the life of Darren and how he handled his illness? Although right now the tragedy appears to be Darren's illness and death, the real tragedy would be to forget the beauty of who Darren was and the message he brings to us. Through him, we have all received a glimpse of heaven."

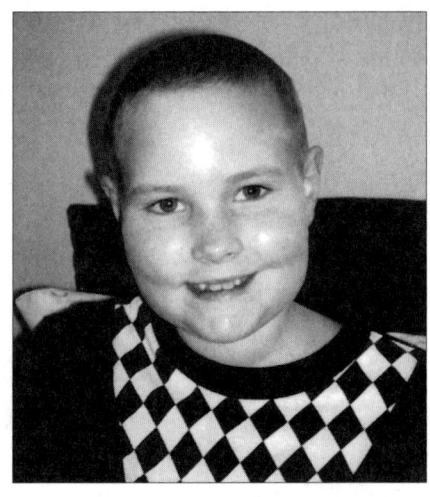

Megan Nelson: 1983–1993

"Will you put my blankey in the casket with me when I die?"

Megan was diagnosed with leukemia in September of 1988 at age five. When she was eight, her leukemia came back. When it appeared her doctors would not be able to get her into remission, her parents included her in all conversations and decisions. Megan decided she didn't want to attempt any more treatment and wanted to go home. Knowing she would probably not live much longer after her second relapse, Megan asked her mother, "Will you put my blankey in the casket with me when I die?" After telling her mother and sister what she wanted them to have, she asked them to give the rest of her possessions "to the poor and homeless."

Megan's parents were exceptionally open and honest with her. Toward the end, when they had gone home so that Megan could be surrounded by familiar things and people, she asked challenging question such as, "Will I be in pain when I die?" They had everyone come in for a last farewell and allowed Megan to do as much or as little as she felt like. They put a bed in the living room for her and surrounded her with activity but also kept her bedroom available for quiet sleep when she needed it. They included her friends as much as possible and took Megan to special events when she was up for it. They gave up worrying about wearing masks. They looked at picture albums together, reviewed fun times, talked openly about death and heaven, and even made funeral arrangements together.

After doing so much to prepare for Megan's death, they were suddenly granted a short-term miracle when Megan had an unexpected, unexplained remission that opened up the possibility of a bone marrow transplant. Her family was prepared for Megan's death but not for having to make this decision. Megan herself was prepared for heaven, which sounded pretty wonderful to her after years of treatment and pain and suffering.

Megan's parents were in a no-win situation. If they did not attempt the transplant, they would always wonder if it might have cured her. After making the agonizing decision to go ahead with the transplant, Megan went from waiting for the arms of Jesus to take her home to the invasive, sterile environment of the bone marrow transplant unit. Unfortunately, instead of dying in comfort in her own bed surrounded by the love of her family, Megan died in the intensive care unit attached to tubes and swollen beyond recognition.

For me, this was an example of how sometimes our attempts to keep people alive at all costs exact a price that is cruel for both patients and families. Fortunately, times have changed over the last twenty-five years. Bone marrow transplants, while still risky, are more successful today than they used to be.

Megan's mom, Mary, is currently writing a book titled *One Body* on their experiences during Megan's illness. Like my book, it has had several stops and starts, but I look forward to reading it when it's published.

Kirk Zuhone: 1983–2015

"I would like to get into a time machine and fly right out of here!"

When five-year-old Kirk was diagnosed in July of 1988 with leukemia, his treatment soon became a family affair. Diagnosed with an osteosarcoma that required the amputation of his left leg, his Uncle Doug, a long-term survivor, had been a patient at our oncology unit when he was a teenager. The staff who were around when Doug was treated were pretty upset to see another family member come through our doors.

Besides Dan and Shelley, Kirk's parents, his paternal grandparents, Art and Charlotte, were present at the hospital for most of Kirk's treatments. John and Megan, his siblings, also visited frequently. Shelly's parents played a key role by caring for John and Megan during the many days and nights Dan and Shelly were at the hospital.

I spent a lot of time with the entire family and still see them yearly when they visit our area in Florida. Dan was a very devoted dad and self-admitted "Nervous Nelly," so we spent a lot of time calming him down. He also had a good sense of humor he'd inherited from his dad and a sense of honesty about his quirks, so we also spent a lot of time laughing. Kirk's brother John was brilliant and often appeared to be spaced out. Today, this "spaced out" astrophysicist works with the Chandra X-ray, the world's most powerful X-ray telescope.

During his first three-year bout of chemo, when Kirk was about to start first grade, he didn't want to get out of the car on his first day of school because he was afraid kids would make fun of him. Dan just picked him up and carried him inside. Kirk said, "I would like to get into a time machine and fly right out of here!" Dan, who felt the same way, said, "Can I go with you?"

When Kirk relapsed at age nine, he became aware that his doctors were afraid the chemotherapy wasn't working. Dan recalls that, one day, Kirk got out of bed and started trying to pull out all the IV lines he was connected to. When Dan told him to stop, Kirk said, "What's the difference? I'm going to die anyway!" Dan told him, "I can't promise that you will live, but I'm not going anywhere. I'm going to stay right here with you all the way." Kirk climbed back into bed and didn't say anything more.

During that time, Kirk was again afraid to return to school, and with good reason. As kids get older, they often become less kind, but Kirk had met a new boy in school who had a brother with cerebral palsy. One day another boy said to Kirk, "What's the matter with you? You don't have hair!"

Ryan, the new kid, said, "You leave him alone. He has cancer, and he is my friend!"

From that day on, as far as Kirk was concerned, Ryan walked on water.

Because of his poor response to treatment this time around, Kirk's best chance of survival was a bone marrow transplant.

His brother John was the donor, but he wasn't a perfect match, so the transplant physician was concerned about the potential for a serious side effect called graft-versus-host disease. Another concern was John's life-threatening allergies. Would Kirk acquire John's allergies along with his bone marrow?

The first day Kirk was allowed to eat real food post-transplant, we had a crash cart waiting outside his room just in case. We all held our breath, but Kirk did okay. He eventually did acquire some of John's allergies but not to the severity his brother suffered.

Kirk did surprisingly well after the transplant. He went on to complete high school and was a music major in college. He played saxophone, wrote music for the church, and helped Dan and Grandpa Art with farming. Unfortunately, when he was twenty-nine, he was diagnosed with a large lipo-sarcoma tumor the size of a football in his stomach. Medical staff told the family they were seeing more and more adults who had been treated for leukemia when they were young being diagnosed with sarcomas. Doctors removed the tumor and resected part of Kirk's stomach, but he developed a serious infection post-surgery and had to battle that first, which delayed the chemo.

Three types of chemotherapy drugs were tried, but none seemed to work. Kirk had to be on TPN (total parenteral nutrition) for months because he was unable to eat. Hospice was called in, but Kirk wanted to try chemo again. He wasn't ready to give up the fight. He stayed positive, hoping for a miracle, and the oncologist was shocked when the new drug worked and the tumor kept shrinking. The medical staff hadn't thought he would survive, but once again he beat the odds.

When Kirk was in the hospital, unable to eat and doing poorly, a doctor asked him, "Is there anything I can do for you?" Kirk replied, "Bring me some chicken from Outback."

Although he laughed, the oncologist didn't think Kirk would survive, let alone eat or drink again.

Responding to Kirk's determination, the staff began giving him a tablespoon of water at a time and gradually increased his intake. Kirk went from being in hospice in June, unable to eat or drink, to eating Thanksgiving dinner with his family. He was even able to eat his beloved Outback chicken.

Nonetheless, from that point on, Kirk was never free of cancer or suffering. Despite this—or perhaps because of this—he became very spiritual and wrote beautiful songs about faith and love. His family said he never once complained.

Al and I saw him for the last time in March of 2014, a year before he died. We were touched at what a good, kind, and insightful young adult he had become and tickled that he had inherited his dad and grandad's quirky sense of humor.

During Kirk's final days, Dan asked him, "Are you afraid to die?"

Kirk said, "No, I am not. I am just not ready."

I found that response typical of children and adults who had defied the odds many times. They were used to fighting for their lives and did not know how and when to let go.

Kirk's strong faith permeated his adult life and shone at his funeral. His band and his sister Megan sang five of the songs Kirk had written and produced. The title of one song, "God Strong," was engraved in the ring Kirk wore. The chorus goes, "We want to be God strong, listen for when He calls. We want to be God strong, by His grace we can hold on."

Another song Kirk wrote titled "This Is the Good Life" contained the following verse: "He listens when we cry out in prayer, to the very end of the age He'll be there. He'll be found whenever we seek him. He'll be our strength when we need him."

Kirk wrote most of that song from his hospital bed, and his inspiration for how to handle adversity with grace lives on, especially in his songs.

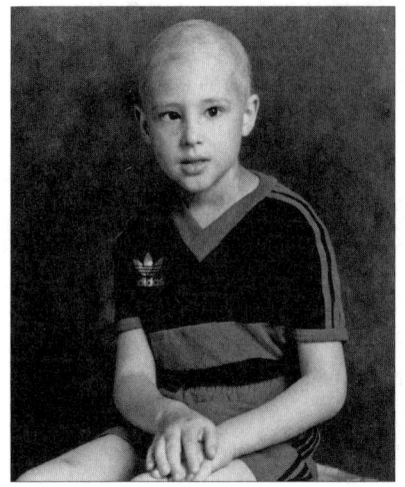 

Andrew Peter: 1978–1987 *(left)*

Matthew Peter: 1982–1990 *(right)*

"Both boys were buried in their favorite attire…"

Andrew and Matt both had leukemia. Born four years apart, they were more than brothers; they were best buddies. After Andrew died in 1987 at age nine, his younger brother Matt never found the key to being fully happy again until he joined his big brother in 1990.

Andrew, the older brother, had two relapses. After his second relapse, he played Little League until six days before he died. He made three hits and caught the last out of his last game. He died in his daddy's arms wearing a T-shirt and blue jeans and was aware until the end.

Matt, who relapsed when he was eight, was outside riding his bike and playing backyard ball until four days before he died. The day he died, he asked to go to the farm with his daddy. They stayed for fifteen minutes, and on the ride home in the pickup truck, he talked normally one minute, tried to say the same phrase over and over the next, and then fell asleep. No pain…No fear. He died in his daddy's arms, wearing a T-shirt and blue jeans, just like his big brother Andrew.

Both boys were buried in their favorite attire, a St. Louis Cardinals T-shirt and blue jeans with a ball glove in their caskets.

Left to right: Tori Nichols, Matthew Peter, and Andrew Peter

Sadly, both of the boys' parents have joined the boys in heaven. Their mom died in 1994 of breast cancer and their dad in 2014 of a heart attack. Their sister, Tori Nichols *(pictured above with her brothers)*, is now in the medical field doing cardiac ultrasounds. I told Tori she turned out to be an amazing young woman in spite of all the tragedies in her family, but perhaps it was because of them.

Janalee and Emily Kreft

Emily Kreft: survivor

"...and together we can beat this awful war."

Exceptionally pretty and talented twelve-year-old Emily was being treated for leukemia. After a relapse, she had a bone marrow transplant. A very creative child who wrote poems during her treatment and created a picture book, Emily was endowed with artistic talent like her mother, Tami. Each day that Emily was in the bone marrow transplant unit, her mother drew a picture and sayings on the whiteboard in the room such as, "Everything's coming up roses on day 29" with a picture of roses growing.

Both Emily and her mother used their talents to try to make other children going through treatment happy. In March of 1994, fifteen months after her bone marrow transplant, Emily was able to meet the woman who had donated her bone marrow so that Emily could live. It was a happy and tearful event for Emily, her parents, and for Pennie Ahearn of Flint, Michigan. The following is an excerpt from one of my favorite poems that Emily wrote at age twelve:

> ## Put Your Hand in Mine
>
> *So the road's a little longer,*
>
> *the stream's a little wider,*
>
> *and there seems to be a*
>
> *boulder that wasn't there before.*
>
> *That doesn't bother me.*
>
> *Just put your hand in mine*
>
> *and we will walk a little farther,*
>
> *jump a little more, and together*
>
> *we can beat this awful war.*

On the last week of my employment at St. Louis Children's Hospital, Emily and her mother made a life-size cake and presented it to me on a gurney. Emily also made me colorful earrings of children dancing that I still have and painted the cover of a beautiful album. Al and I attended her celebration party after her successful transplant.

Despite her beauty, charm, and talent, life is challenging for Emily, who is now thirty-seven years old. On the positive side, she received a master's degree in art therapy and has had a private practice in art therapy and counseling. She also adopted a daughter, Stella, who is six years old and the light of her life. Emily's medical challenges include heart complications from her earlier treatment, thyroid cancer, and recently breast cancer. On top of her medical issues, Emily was recently divorced. As she wrote in the last part of her poem "Put Your Hand in Mine":

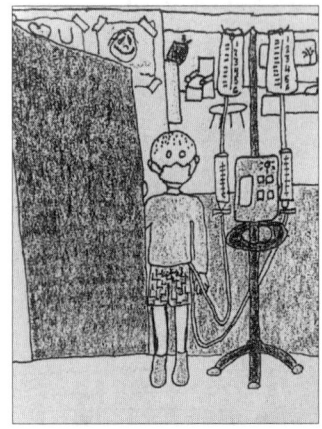

> **Rain is falling,**
> *the thunder never stops.*
> *There's a dark cloud*
> *over my head but*
> *I will not let it stay.*
> *The rain surrounds me.*
> *I throw some seeds*
> *I have gathered along the path.*
> *Beautiful flowers now surround me.*
> *The sun shines down*
> *and warms me from the rain.*
> *The rainbow comes out at last!*

I know that with Emily's wonderful spirit and courage, the rainbow will eventually come out and the sun will shine down on her again.

Nafeesa Scales with her mother Barbara

Nafeesa Scales: 1978–1989

"...these ministers might be able to wash the guilt from their hands, but they can't wash it from their souls."

Eight-year-old Nafeesa was diagnosed in October of 1986 with neuroblastoma and had tumors in both her stomach and left lung. She relapsed in January of 1989 and died the following New Year's Eve at age eleven.

Nafeesa's treatment was extremely difficult, and her mom, Barbara, was a single parent with no family to help. Barb worked as a phlebotomist at a local private hospital, and Nafeesa was her only child.

Inexplicably, I often found that the least sympathetic employers worked in the medical system. Barb's employer was not very understanding about her need to frequently take off work, so I often advocated for her. Her employer said she could have an unpaid sick leave for three months, but Barb couldn't afford this. In addition, if she took the time off, the hospital could not guarantee that she could return to the same or a similar job. Finally, if Barb left and returned, she would have to start over on the hospital's pay scale, a major sacrifice after fifteen years on the job.

Barb eventually quit her job to care for Nafeesa when she was terminal and needed full-time care. This period, Barb recalls, was "pure hell."

On top of all the care Nafeesa required when she became wheelchair dependent, Barb suffered significant back pain and at times became immobilized herself. Despite her own trials, Barb did all she could to help Nafeesa squeeze every possible bit of joy out of her eleven years of life. In addition, Barb somehow maintained a great sense of humor that often had me vacillating between laughter and tears.

In spite of the topnotch medical care Nafeesa received and support from her church where Nafeesa participated in choir and attended Sunday School, Barb sometimes took Nafeesa to "faith healers." Desperate to save her daughter, she sometimes got stuck between her practical side and the message from the "healers" that if she had sufficient faith and prayed hard enough, Nafeesa would be cured.

I heard variations on this theme from different ministers throughout my ten years at St. Louis Children's Hospital. When the loved one died, the minister felt righteous while the family was further forever burdened.

How unfair! Sometimes, no matter how hard someone prays, how strongly they believe, or how much they love, their loved one dies. Family members are then stricken with a sense of guilt on top of their grief. As far as I'm concerned, these ministers might be able to wash the guilt from their hands, but they can't wash it from their souls.

At a support program for kids with cancer in April of 1989, I asked Nafeesa how she felt about death. She said, "I'm scared to leave my mom behind who will miss me so much, but I will be happy to be free from pain and in heaven, safe and happy, able to look down at Earth and watch over my mother and friends."

Because she hated the hospital so much, we arranged for Nafeesa to die at home with the support of a home care nurse. Three days before she died, as Barb was leaving for a doctor's appointment, she started to give Nafeesa a quick goodbye hug, but Nafeesa wouldn't let go of her neck.

Suddenly Nafeesa's nose started bleeding and she began to seize. By the time they got her to the hospital, she was in a coma. Barb stayed by her side until Nafeesa died, three days later, on New Year's Eve.

Nafeesa Scales

The anniversary of a death is always a hard, sad time, but when it comes on a holiday or another day that is special to the family, it makes that day even harder.

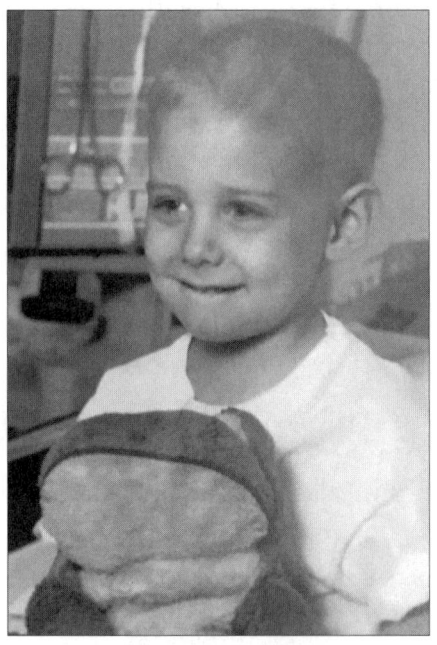

Jordan Rupe-Smith: survivor

"He would sit on my lap and explain the world as he saw it."

Jordan had blonde hair and big brown eyes with the longest dark lashes I'd ever seen. He was diagnosed at age two with B cell lymphoma, which at that time was a rare and deadly type of cancer with a poor survival rate. Eventually his hair and eyelashes fell out and he became pale and thin due to his very aggressive treatment, but he never lost his cute personality.

Jordan was exceptionally smart and articulate for his age, so during the times he was getting his outpatient treatment, I always enjoyed having him come into my office to get his "prize" after his fingerstick for his blood counts. He would sit on my lap and explain the world as he saw it. Jordan was especially interested in the Teenage Mutant Ninja Turtles and Ghostbusters, and he often wore these costumes to the clinic.

Jordan's parents had agreed to a new experimental and very aggressive treatment, so he spent a lot of time in the hospital. Night after night, his mom, Pat, slept on the narrow window seat in the hospital. By day, she did all she could to create some fun for Jordan and the other children. An architect by trade, Pat also became a board member of our parents' group, CURE, while her mother, Norma Rupe, became my dearest volunteer. Despite Jordan's nausea, mouth sores, joint pains, fevers, and headaches, he was a joy to be around, as were his mother and grandmother. Some people just shine no matter what their circumstances.

Jordan is a survivor despite all the odds, but when he was twelve and his brother, Sammy, was ten, Pat died in a car accident. She was divorced from the boys' father, and after her death, they went to live with their dad.

Norma began visiting me in Florida as she tried to deal with her grief over losing Pat. She ended up becoming my best volunteer at the national Prader-Willi Syndrome Association when I was the executive director, and she was my dear friend until she died in 2009. With her sunny disposition, generosity of spirit, and willingness to try anything, Norma was my role model of how to grow old. I still have a special box of handmade Christmas ornaments made by Pat and Norma. I hang them on my tree every holiday, and I often picture Norma in heaven, dancing with our grandson, Adam, and all the children with cancer whose lives she touched.

Al and I still keep in touch with Jordan, who is the head manager of a theater in St. Louis. I was happy to hear he will be married this coming spring. We are also the key support people for his ninety-six-year-old grandfather, Bill, paying it forward as a thank you to Norma for all the volunteer work she did for me.

Vignettes

The following short vignettes offer a glimpse of the preciousness of these sweet, courageous, sometimes funny, sometimes sad children I had the privilege to work with. I have lost touch with their parents, but I would love to hear from them if they recognize their child's story.

Justin, age nine

"Jan, you better cover your ears. I scream pretty bad!"

Justin was sobbing because he had just been told by Dr. Wall that he had relapsed again. Suddenly he stopped crying and asked, "Does this mean I'll get prizes again?"

He was referring to the prize shelves in my office. When I affirmed that he would, Justin warned me, "You know I'm a lot older now, so I am more particular."

Later that day, we had to start torturing Justin again with a bone marrow aspirate, spinal tap, and numerous needle sticks.

He forewarned me, "Jan, you had better get out of here."

When I told him I wasn't leaving, that I was going to stay with him all the way, Justin said, "Becky [a nurse], you had better take my legs. Jan, you better cover your ears. I scream pretty bad!"

Tyler, age six

"As I stepped out of the car, there at my feet lay a small red stuffed Cardinal bird..."

Sometimes my glimpse of heaven came through something a child or teen would say just before they died. Sometimes it came through an extraordinary experience.

Tyler was a handsome brown-eyed boy with a sweet smile who was almost inseparable from his Cardinals baseball cap. Diagnosed with Wilms tumor, he died at age six after a lengthy illness. My husband and I went to his visitation and found the room filled with Cardinals baseball memorabilia.

Afterwards, Al drove me back to the hospital and dropped me off at the busy front entrance. As I stepped out of the car, there at my feet lay a small red stuffed Cardinal bird with lifelike feathers.

Where had it come from? I felt it was a message from Tyler that he was okay. That bird still hangs on our Christmas tree twenty-four years later.

Bobbie, age eight

"Don't tell my heart, my achy breaky heart..."

Although most of the children I worked with had wonderful, dedicated families, there were sad exceptions. One of them was little Bobbie, who had acute lymphocytic leukemia and eventually a bone marrow transplant. It was a struggle to be assured he would get to treatment and even more of a struggle to get his mother to visit. Often, Bobbie would cry, saying, "She promised to come!" or "I knew she wouldn't come!"

Because Bobbie was often alone, my husband, Al, became his official volunteer. When Bobbie was isolated in the transplant unit, Al brought him a tape player and headset. Bobbie loved country-western music, and when Al asked what tapes he wanted, it broke our hearts when Bobbie said, "My Achy Breaky Heart" and "Where Am I Going to Live When I Get Home?"

Bobbie died while still in the transplant unit, so he didn't have to worry about where he was going to live when he went home—he went to a better home in heaven.

Eric, age seven

"Mom, which wish is more important?"

Eric was being treated for leukemia. At the time, this diagnosis meant an automatic three years of chemotherapy.

One day, he and his mother, Janet, were throwing pennies in a fountain when Eric said, "What did you wish for, Mom?"

Janet said, "I wished your leukemia would never come back."

Eric said, "I wished I would go to heaven."

He pondered that for a minute, then tugged on his mother's shirt and asked, "Mom, which wish is more important?"

She answered, "I guess yours is, Eric."

I do not know if Eric survived his leukemia, but I treasure a copy of the card that Jenny, Eric's sister, made for the kids in the bone marrow transplant unit. It said, "God please let these kids have a chans. I'll try to help the kanser kids. I'll try so heard—so don't give up and do your best. Try heard and you'll servive I hope. I'll pray for you so you can grow up and live for a long time. I love you all. And even if you die, I'll pray for you and I'll ask God to take care of you."

Alexis, age two

"...Alexis knew that after her finger stick, she would get a prize from my office."

Most of our little patients dreaded getting their finger stuck in the lab for blood counts, but Alexis was an exception. My office was next to the lab, and one day Alexis came to my door worried because the lab door was locked and she couldn't get in.

Most kids would have smiled with relief, but Alexis knew that after her finger stick, she would get a prize from my office. After I arranged for the door to be unlocked, Alexis bounced up in the chair and stuck out her finger with a big smile.

I returned to my office, but a few minutes later, I heard her sobbing. Puzzled, I went to see what was wrong.

Two-year-old Alexis was crying because the lab was out of Beauty and the Beast Band-Aids and she had to wear another cartoon character!

Sarah, age two

"No, I'm an angel."

Two-year-old Sarah loved to wear princess outfits. One day after her bone marrow transplant, I asked her, "Are you a princess?"

She had always responded "Yes!" in the past, but this time, she surprised us all by saying, "No, I'm an angel."

The next day, the doctors discovered she had relapsed. Sweet Sarah died shortly thereafter.

Stephanie, age five

"...I couldn't grant every wish."

Hard as I tried, I couldn't grant every wish.

When I was talking to five-year-old Stephanie about the possibility of taking a special "wish trip," she asked, "Can I ask for anything?"

When I asked what she wanted to wish for, she said, "Can I wish to live forever?"

I had many tough questions to answer, and I don't know which was worse, answering a small child or answering a teenager.

Then again, I didn't have to choose.

As much as I loved working with the younger children, much of my time was spent working with their families. They needed their parents much more than they needed me, so I needed to be their parents' sounding board and advocate.

My role with some of the preteens and teenagers was different; they often needed a sounding board and support system independent of their parents. At a time when they should have been spreading their wings, their wings were often clipped because of their treatment and their parent's fears.

Also, the teens did not have the innocence of the young children. They knew their lives were in danger, and they knew they were different from their peers. As the next few chapters reveal, in many ways, the teenagers were my biggest challenge and my greatest joy. My bonds with them were often strong once I broke through the tough veneer guarding the vulnerability within.

And Then There Were Nine

*T*he stories in this chapter are based on just a few of the teenagers whose lives and deaths have forever become part of who I am and what I believe. Their suffering was unfair and tragic. To not share their strength, beauty, and profoundness would add to the unfairness and tragedy. This chapter is dedicated to them and to all the special teenagers who shared their hopes, fears, anger, tears, and crazy sense of humor with me.

In September of 1991, our support group for teens with cancer went to see "one of our own," Corey Peterson, who was starring in the play *Ten Little Indians*. In this play, one by one, the key character's lives are suddenly snuffed out by a mysterious killer.

Corey had recently rebounded after completing yet another round of chemotherapy. He had already been through two relapses of his neuroblastoma, a cancer of the peripheral nervous system, as well as a bone marrow transplant. We all spent the evening rejoicing over our "star's" comeback and his new head of hair.

After the play, we held a sleepover at our home for the teens. My husband, Al, and I had rented a movie starring two teenage girls with cancer, and the group enjoyed critiquing its inaccuracy regarding the real world of teenagers with cancer, a world they knew all too well.

When the group realized there were ten teens spending the night, they began joking about who the mysterious murderer would target next. Looking around the room, I reflected on how special each of "my" teens were, and I basked in the joy that each was doing well at the moment. Unfortunately, my period of peace disappeared the next morning with the moon and the stars.

As I was cooking breakfast, Corey privately mentioned to me that he was having trouble keeping food down but did not want to see the doctor until the play was over. My heart sank as I gave him a hug. His initial tumor had been wrapped around his intestines, and we both knew without speaking what this probably meant. Two days later, during his clinic visit, Corey's world came crashing down for the fourth and final time. The "mysterious killer," cancer, took charge of his life again. That day, as I grieved with Corey and his parents, I was struck by the similarities between the play and how the teens in our group lived, never knowing if and when the elusive killer would strike again.

The following stories pay tribute to these special teens.

Corey Peterson, 1973–1992

*"...with the trumpet in one hand
and a bucket in the other..."*

Although he had a good wit, Corey was one of the more serious teens in our group. He was born in Seoul, Korea, in 1973 and adopted when he was sixteen months old. When he arrived at the airport in the United States, his parents, Pam and Pete Peterson, said he weighed only twelve pounds. He was emaciated and sickly but had a fighting spirit even then, and his parents were told he charmed everyone on the plane.

Corey made outstanding achievements in his short eighteen years despite being diagnosed with neuroblastoma at age fifteen and enduring three relapses that involved chemotherapy, radiation, and multiple surgeries. With superhuman grit and determination, Corey managed to be involved with student government, the school band as drum major, all state choir, space camp, drama club, engineering club, Boy Scouts, church choir, and Lifesavers Club. Often, the chemotherapy needle would barely be out of his arm before he was off to play in the band with the trumpet in one hand and a bucket in the other in case he became nauseated. Corey also won the Silver Alpha and American Legion awards for stellar academics.

For several months during Corey's illness, he could not eat and survived by intravenous TPN, total parenteral nutrition, treatments. Of course, he desperately longed to eat food, so when he was finally able to do so, we had a "Corey Peterson Pig-Out Party" at our home complete with his favorite foods, balloons and posters, and his friends from the teen treatment group. They had a lot of fun eating and drinking around the pool and sharing the dark humor only allowed amongst their inner circle of fellow teenage cancer sufferers. For example, the girls could make fun of the times they were mistaken for a boy due to their bald heads, but beware the outsider who would make fun of them!

It was interesting but not surprising when Corey's straight black hair grew back very curly after chemotherapy. Often, hair color changed, thin hair came back thicker (unless there was radiation to the head), straight hair became curly, and so on. When my own hair grew back after chemotherapy, I had a head full of ringlets for the first time in my life.

Corey said that what kept him going was having something to look forward to. He wanted to apply for the Walt Disney World Illinois Dreamer and Doer award in May of 1991, but he was writhing in pain and we were up against a deadline for the application. I finally told him, "Corey, just dictate to me and I will write it for you." Al and I stayed at the hospital typing until midnight the night before the deadline in order to get it in on time, and Corey won! Traveling to Disneyworld with his family and receiving special recognition was one more thing that gave him the impetus to keep going.

After his latest relapse, Corey's best option was a bone marrow transplant. When he was in the bone marrow transplant unit, I tried to think of ways to cheer him up. Corey and some of the other boys in the group often kidded about going to Hooters someday, so I asked my husband if he would go to Hooters and try to talk a couple of the waitresses into visiting Corey in the transplant unit. At this point, Corey was allowed visitors in his isolation room if they were not sick and if they took the necessary precautions. It was getting near the date he would be able to get out of the unit, and he wasn't at as great of a risk for infection, so I queried a couple of Corey's closest friends about my plan. They were more than happy to participate, so they visited Corey while I met the Hooters girls in the front lobby.

You can imagine the attention we drew as Al and I took the girls up to the ninth floor wearing their skimpy bare midriff tops with "Hooters" written across their chests and their signature orange short shorts! This was not a typical sight in a children's hospital. Of course, Corey was delighted, as were his friends, who made sure they appeared in the pictures we took.

Despite Corey's extraordinary courage and ability to bounce back, each time he relapsed, the odds against his survival became greater. Corey loved politics and history, and his biggest dream besides the dream of surviving was to visit Washington, DC. In January of 1992, we helped arrange this through Operation Liftoff. Off to DC he went, in a wheelchair, with tubes in his chest, and morphine patches on his body to control his pain. In addition to receiving chemotherapy by IV in the hotel room, Corey met Vice President Dan Quayle during a special tour of the White House, visited the aerospace museum, and toured the headquarters of the FBI.

Corey was a key member of our teens with cancer support group. During one of our meetings, we talked about what we ultimately want out of life when we die. Aside from the general kidding, the consensus among the teens was that they wanted people to remember them with respect and love. Corey felt comforted knowing that people would remember him this way. At the same time, he believed that if he worked hard enough, he could do anything and overcome any obstacle, including cancer. Nonetheless, he felt the pain of losing his "normal" friends because he was so often out of circulation due to his treatment and side effects. Corey said, "I don't like losing my friends—and I don't particularly like losing myself either."

In February of 1992, nearly one thousand Alton High School students rallied around him for Corey Peterson Day. Even after all the relapses and his very difficult chemotherapy, Cory managed to graduate high school. That June, two months before his death, he walked across the stage to receive his diploma. Even though he had to be pushed up next to the stage in a wheelchair, Corey managed that walk to the cheers of his classmates and the tears of his parents, his sister Robin, and Al and me.

Towards the end of his life, Corey told me that as much as he loved living, he was not afraid to die. His biggest concern was leaving his mom, dad, and sister with their pain and sorrow. Corey told me that he used to be ashamed of his parents because they didn't make a lot of money, but through the course of his illness, his attitude had completely changed. He realized his parents were devoted to him and were always there to support him.

Pam and Pete were not only there for Corey but also for many other kids whose parents were unable to be at the hospital. Corey was the light of their lives from the day he got off the plane from Seoul as a baby to the day he died in his mom's arms at age nineteen.

I am grateful to be able to say that Corey's inspiration and his parents' dedication still shines through his sister, Robin Granger. Also adopted from Korea, she is the proud mother of children of all shades of color. She has helped raise four stepchildren, adopted three children, and is a foster parent. She is the director of compassionate ministry at her church and oversees multiple programs to help others. The light of Corey lives on in her.

Jason Council: 1975–1991

"Jason's last wishes were to...have a magician perform at his funeral to make people laugh."

Jason was a fair-haired young man with a golden personality whose diagnosis of osteogenic sarcoma in February of 1990 at age fifteen required his left leg to be amputated.

Jason's passion was performing magic. His stepdad, Larry, even came up with a stage name for him, "The CharisMagic Kid," a word play combining Jason's charismatic personality with his magic talent.

After a few relapses, knowing he was dying, Jason asked me for three things. Of course, I was determined to honor all three wishes. After all, I had already "delivered" on a few other wishes, including helping him get a job. This had not been easy given that he was fifteen, had only one leg, had metastasis to the lungs, and was being treated with chemotherapy.

Jason's last wishes were to get his driver's license, to soak in a hot tub, and to have a magician perform at his funeral to make people laugh.

Helping Jason get his driver's license on his sixteenth birthday, ten days before he died, was one of my biggest challenges. At that time, Jason was on oxygen full-time due to the widespread metastasis to his lungs as well as heavy doses of morphine. Because he could no longer wear his artificial leg, he was in a wheelchair.

The first person I talked to at the driver's license bureau thought I was crazy and told me, "No way!" Of course, this man was unnerved by the thought of the behind-the-wheel test, but it was also clear that no one in the department of transportation understood the philosophy that "rules are meant to be smiled at."

Having a son of my own, Matt, with a rare disorder, Prader-Willi syndrome, I had long ago learned to scale the brick walls of the system, so all this meant was that I was going to have to put on my climbing gear.

After going through many calls and personnel within the system, I found out who had the power to make exceptions to rules. This courageous supervisor assigned Jason the most foolhardy/courageous driving instructor in all of St. Louis.

When the big day came, we carried Jason to the car to take the test on a very quiet road in a very quiet neighborhood. Jason skipped a dose of morphine in order to be sufficiently alert, his mother, Melanie, sat in the back to monitor his oxygen, and he passed!

In a desperate attempt to physically place Jason's license in his hands before he died, I explained the situation to the Missouri Highway Patrol, which rushed the request through the department and assigned a patrolman to drive the license from Jefferson City to St. Louis, a two-hour drive, to personally hand it to Jason on his birthday.

And Then There Were Nine

We had arranged a birthday party at Jason's home that night with all his friends from the teen support group and a magician to entertain everyone. Forlornly, Jason told his friends he hadn't passed the test. Everyone was offering condolences when, with a magician's flair and a big smile, Jason produced from thin air the receipt that verified he'd passed. The party went on jubilantly from there except for the many quiet tears that were shed as we sang to Jason, knowing this would be the last birthday he would celebrate. Jason insisted on staying up in his wheelchair until the end. While the magician entertained everyone, Jason dozed contentedly.

Jason's second request was to get into a hot tub because he longed to feel warm water against his body. He had been too sick and weak to stand in the shower for several weeks, so sponge baths were part of his daily care. Knowing that any public place with a jacuzzi would freak out at the sight of this thin, pale teenager being carried into their facility minus a leg, on oxygen, and with very flaky skin, I called our oldest daughter, Tina Kiel. She and her husband, John, readily agreed to let Jason soak in their hot tub, so I took nurse Barb Carr, my sidekick in "adventures of the heart with dying children," with me to monitor Jason's oxygen and medication.

I carried Jason into Tina's and John's hot tub while Barb held the oxygen tubes and the IV morphine pump lines out of the way. With his eyes closed, Jason smiled and said with a contented sigh, "Water never felt so good in all my life!"

Jason's third request was to have a magician perform at his funeral so that it "wasn't all sad." Since this was not a wish most magicians would be comfortable with, I called my friends at Wishing Well. They connected me with Slick Rick, who had donated his services for fundraising benefits in the past. Rick had also performed at Jason's birthday party, and he assured Jason that he would honor his wishes at his memorial service. In addition, Jason's stepfather, Larry, arranged to have one of the most esteemed magicians in the region, Harry Monte, perform a Broken Wand ceremony at Jason's service.

The Broken Wand ceremony is one of the highest tributes given to a magician after his or her death, and Jason was touched and honored by this gesture. His only regret, he told me, was that he would not be there to see it.

As he had hoped to do, Jason died at home, free of pain, and his funeral was filled with wonderful testimonies of his life and magic tricks with Harry Monte performing the Broken Wand ceremony and Slick Rick doing the magic show in a side visitation room. We all envisioned Jason smiling down on us and nodding with approval at this final performance.

Denise Woodson: 1970–1985

"Denise was walking down the hall with her IV pole, saying she was quitting treatment and leaving..."

Denise, a beautiful fourteen-year-old African-American girl, was one of my first patients. If life circumstances had been different, she could have been a model. Denise, nicknamed NeCee, and her sister, Rochelle, were raised by their mother. Ella Woodson was a sweet woman who made her living reupholstering furniture for a small company. They lived in a small home in a neighborhood near the airport.

When Denise was first diagnosed with acute myelogenous leukemia, a type of leukemia that is more common in teens and also more difficult to cure, she told me she was unable to sleep. After she began to trust me, she confided that she was afraid she might die in her sleep. Of course, as professionals, we all knew that young people do not die of cancer without any warning soon after diagnosis, but how would a naïve, terrified young woman know this unless someone told her?

I asked Denise to write down any more questions or concerns she had so we could discuss them and alleviate her fears. I still have her questions:

- Will I get to play any games?
- Will my whole life change?
- Will I get my weight back?
- Can I get rid of this disease?
- Will I die?
- When I get home, will it be the same? I mean, will I be treated the same?
- How long will my side effects last?
- How long will my treatments be?
- Will my friends still like me?
- What if my mother and sister catch a cold when I get home? Will they have to wear a mask?

I quickly learned that there weren't easy answers to many of the questions my teens asked. One of the things I said to them, starting with Denise, was, "I will try to answer you honestly, but before you ask the question, make sure you want to know the answer."

Eventually, I learned that teenagers typically wanted honest answers to day-to-day questions such as will it hurt, will my hair fall out, and so on, but they did not want statistics about their chances of survival unless the odds were good. Usually, they also wanted a ray of hope, but each teen was different so I had to get to know their individual way of coping. I would typically throw out "feeler" questions such as, "What did the doctor tell you? What do you think is happening?" The answers to a few choice questions would tell me how honest to be or how lightly to tread.

During my early years with pediatric oncology, when the side effects of chemotherapy were especially gruesome, I had many challenges with teens. It wasn't unusual for a nurse to come get me because a teenager had locked herself in the clinic bathroom just before treatment was to start or for a parent to call from home and tell me her son had locked himself in his bedroom and refused to come out to go to treatment. I got pretty good at talking through doors, even over the phone.

One afternoon, I received a panicked call from the oncology unit. Denise was walking down the hall with her IV pole, saying she was quitting treatment and leaving and that no one could stop her. She was due to have a lumbar puncture, often called a spinal tap, and this procedure was always difficult, creating anxiety for her and for the doctor who had to perform it. Spinal taps detect leukemia in the central nervous system by collecting and testing the cerebrospinal fluid surrounding the brain and spinal cord. This was before the wonder drug Versed came along, giving patients total amnesia throughout the procedure.

I talked Denise into sitting in the waiting room and discreetly waived security away. After I let Denise vent her fears and anger, I asked if she had thought about the consequences of not getting the needed testing and chemotherapy. I acknowledged that she might die even if she did get it, but I reminded her that she was certain to die, barring a miracle, if she did not. I then asked her to seriously think about whether she was willing to pay that price.

Denise sat quietly for a moment, then quietly asked if I would stay with her and hold her hand during the procedure. We walked back to her room hand in hand, and I remember wishing she were a little child I could cradle in my arms. Instead, Denise was one of the first of many children and teenagers I had to help grow up long before her time.

Denise's devoted mother took as much time off from work as she dared, which wasn't much, and her younger sister and father loved her very much. Her sister Rochelle, younger than Denise by two years, stated, "Our family members including myself didn't have the proper tools, guidance, or knowledge regarding her cancer or how to be the most supportive. It truly devasted our family when she was diagnosed."

Her relatives were afraid that if they visited her in the hospital, they might give her an infection, a common worry among family members. Denise was being treated before I started the teen group, so she did not have sufficient peer support. She was in the eighth grade, and kids at that age typically don't know how to be helpful, but her classmates did all cheer for her when she received her diploma. There was also a large group of visitors on her fifteenth birthday, which she had to celebrate in the hospital, and we were able to help her mom with funding to throw her a real birthday party when she was released.

Denise was not inundated with gifts like some children who have cancer, so she appreciated any little gift I was able to give her from the "prize" shelves I had installed and had stocked by generous volunteers shortly after I started at the children's hospital. The outpatient unit was new and pristine but sterile looking, so one of my goals was to make it more kid friendly. Denise was also more than eager to go with Al and me to community events when she was able. I also helped arrange a trip for Denise, her sister, and mom to Disney World through one of the wish groups. It was the first time any of them had ever been on an airplane. Like all kids, NeCee (Denise's nickname) and Rochelle fought over the window seat.

How special was this trip? Rochelle recalled, "We were so amazed at how things looked that far up! There was a time we went swimming when NeCee went under the water, and when she came up, her wig slid off. I immediately covered her with my body so she could put it back on! It was a time for us to be sisters and enjoy having fun with each other and our mother."

More recently, Rochelle wrote to me and expressed a familiar theme—her lifelong regret that she wasn't with her sister when she passed away. She wrote, "The day NeCee passed, I did not arrive at the hospital until after she died. It was two days after Thanksgiving, probably around 7:00 p.m. My mother, her father, my aunts, and plenty of family were there already. Some of them had spent the night with her. I had spent the night Thanksgiving Eve and

Thanksgiving Day. I went home because we were all so excited to see her eat ice cream. I fed it to her. We thought this meant she was getting better! After I left, I wasn't made aware that she took a turn for the worse. My cousin Beverly came and picked me up saying NeCee wasn't going to make it. She was driving so fast and it was raining so hard that we almost got into an accident. As soon as we got there, my cousin Lamont said, 'It's too late. She's gone.'

"We ran into her room, and she was lying there with her mouth open and her eyes rolled back. We all started crying and began to shake her, telling her to come back. I remember telling her, 'Don't leave me! I need you!' All the machines were disconnected. Everyone was crying in disbelief. At that moment, I did not accept her death. In tears, I told my mother and her father that NeCee was coming home. We were not leaving her there. I was twelve. I still wanted her to come home even though she was dead."

I have often heard from Rochelle and others how much they regret that their parents were not more honest about how critically ill their sibling was or told them their sibling was nearing death. They now know their parents were trying to protect them from pain, but they all wish they had known more and had been with their sibling at their time of passing. Being protected from short-term pain often created lifelong regret.

I really loved that beautiful shy teen, but I too was unable to be at Denise's side when she passed away on November 30, 1985, as I was away for the Thanksgiving holiday.

She had to take that final walk without me, and I had to live with the reality that I could not be everything to everyone—not an easy thing to accept when the stakes are so high.

Kris Sellberg and Eddie Greenhill

Eddie Greenhill: 1973–1999

"I would have been a hoodlum if I had not gotten cancer."

Eddie was a dark-haired, solidly built Caucasian male with beautiful blue eyes. He was diagnosed shortly before his fourteenth birthday with synovial sarcoma, a cancer that affects the bone, blood, and tissue. It was in his left foot and ankle, making it necessary to amputate his leg below the knee. He spent the remaining thirteen years of his life dealing with relapses—seven in all—and helping teach others not only how to cope but also how to find joy.

At age sixteen, Eddie suffered a relapse. This time the cancer was in his left lung. After about a year of treatment, the doctors found a massive tumor encapsulated in blood just inside his skull, pressing on an occipital lobe. At age nineteen, he relapsed again in the lung, which required intense treatment and the removal of half his left lung. He also had a bone marrow transplant.

Eddie had an amazing ability to bounce back after each setback. Despite all he went through, he had a great sense of humor. A key member of our teen support group, Eddie was known for saying, "I would have been a hoodlum if I had not gotten cancer." He also said that he believed growing up with cancer helped him mature more quickly and gain a better perspective on life.

There was something really cool about Eddie, with his bald head wrapped in a red bandanna, his gait a bit of a swagger, a big smile on his face. The young teens with cancer all looked up to him.

In personal conversations with me and in sharing sessions with the teen group, Eddie talked honestly about what he was going through. During his first round with cancer, he said he was able to maintain a strong sense of denial for several months. He was so confident that nothing would change in his life that on his first day of treatment, he enjoyed a Diet Coke and slice of pizza. Needless to say, it took him over a year before he could face pizza again!

During his first relapse, denial came in a different form, and he was determined to keep up the pace he had in the past, hanging out with friends and going to school, but eventually he realized he needed the support of people who understood what he was going through.

By his second relapse, Eddie was struggling more. He was forced to deal with more critical issues and with the reality of potentially dying. Inside his home, he had to drag himself on the ground to get around because he could no longer wear his artificial leg and because the wheelchair was too big for the house. He said, "I felt almost subhuman, not because of how my parents treated me—they gave me all the love and support in the world—but by the being I had become."

He also had to deal with anger he hadn't felt in the past. Much of the anger focused on how he had just gotten his life back together—he'd gained back his weight, his hair had grown back, and he'd reentered daily life—only to have it all stripped away again. He was angry at the doctors, at God, and at himself. He also became depressed due to the side effects of his treatment. His first treatments were performed on an out-patient basis so he did not have to stay in the hospital for long periods of time, but his mom had to work in order to keep their insurance. In order to reduce his vomiting and head pain, Eddie found he needed total silence, very little light, and to have the house devoid of all smells. This meant he sat in a dark room for several days at a time feeling rotten, vomiting, and isolated. Eventually, he began vomiting simply in anticipation of going in for chemotherapy, not an unusual response, according to the other teens. Eventually, Eddie was able to rise above the agonies of treatment, release his anger, and adjust to his "new normal."

Eddie engaged in his fair share of bargaining throughout treatment. Sometimes he would bargain with his parents for small luxuries, and he would bargain with the doctors and nurses who wanted to protect him to allow him to stretch his limits and experience newer and somewhat riskier life experiences. Much of the bargaining during the last cycle of treatment was with the hospital staff, bargaining for a more normal life through a self-selected schedule of treatment. Eddie told me, "God and I sat at the bargaining table many times. I would say, if you do this or make that happen, then I will do/not do this..." He added, "This kind of bargaining made sense to me—it was a 'you scratch my back and I'll scratch yours' type of deal. Although it worked with my parents and friends, it had little effect on God."

Despite all the years that his body was ravaged by disease and treatment, Eddie managed to complete high school and then college. His life was also full of adventures such as meeting Harrison Ford and attending our special teen trips. Often, when anyone else would have been hospitalized due to low blood counts or extremely potent chemotherapy, Eddie would convince the doctors to let him go back to school because of a test he didn't want to miss or because he was supposed to be a counselor at a camp for children with cancer. After all, he had already done the impossible: given only a year to live at diagnosis, he had already lived many years longer than predicted.

Eventually, Eddie came to terms with what he had to do to survive. He was one of the initial members of our support group for teens with cancer, and this group of people became very important to him. Eddie said, "This group exposed me to a wide variety of different people. You wouldn't believe how many stereotypes and how much bigotry was destroyed forever due to my participation with the group. We helped each other accept life's tempests through the unique perspectives and life experience we each possessed."

During his final relapse, Eddie was glad there was a large group to share with. He told me there were "more ears to listen, more shoulders to cry upon, and more hearts to care." He added, "This may sound kind of strange, but I am happier having had cancer than I think I would have been without it. The people I met along this path are the most incredible people I have ever met. Due to cancer, I have met more people, gone more places, seen more wonders, experienced more emotion, and gained a more open heart and open view. I have even met the love of my life [another teen with cancer] through these dire life events."

Even after his final relapse, when a physician told him the tumors were wrapped around his spine and that he would never be able to walk again or control his bladder and bowels, Eddie said, "It's okay, Mom. I still have my arms and my head—I'm still me."

Eddie's final triumph was becoming certified as a recreational therapist just two weeks before he died. Despite his medical trauma, including multiple tumors in his brain, he still wanted to take the test. Officials from the National Council for Therapeutic Recreation Certification brought the test to him at the hospital and called to tell him he'd passed with flying colors just days before he died.

Eddie was like a son to me, and he often called me his "second mom." When it was apparent he was dying, I flew back to St. Louis from Florida where we were now living to be with him.

When I asked Eddie what he wanted people to remember about him, Eddie stated, "That I was strong and that I helped people out as much as I could." He also wanted me to tell his mother, Betty, how much he loved her.

Eddie's life was one of great tragedy and greater triumph. As Bernie Siegel, M.D. said, "Getting well is not the only goal. Even more important is learning how to live without fear, to be at peace with life and ultimately death."

It was a joy to be part of Eddie's life. He touched my soul deeply. Although Eddie was not "religious" in the technical sense of the word, he was filled with grace.

Eddie died at home in his mother's arms, and Betty said, "No matter how sick he was or how scared I was, I let him fly, but now it was time for him to be back home in the nest."

Even though Eddie's years were few, he lived a fuller life than anyone I know. I have heard it said that "Life is measured in relationships, not time." If that is true, Eddie died a very old man.

John Randles: survivor

"When Eddie was wheeled out of surgery, John followed his stretcher into intensive care."

John, a fourteen-year-old African-American with a solid build and kind eyes, had a leg amputation due to osteogenic sarcoma, a form of bone cancer. He had been doing well in school and was very involved with sports, but after the amputation, he had to have two more surgeries plus extensive chemotherapy. When I first met him, he was so depressed he would barely say more than a polite "Hi," and when he wasn't in the hospital, he refused to leave his home. His mom, Alethea, said he woke up crying one night, worried that no woman would ever be attracted to a man with half a leg.

Eventually, John became involved with our CURE (Children's United Research Effort) teen group and blossomed to become the most active teen volunteer I had. He volunteered almost every day in the summer and even came in on holidays or when there was no school. John was not afraid to sit quietly at the bedside of a child with cancer who was too sick to talk or to visit with the parent of a newly diagnosed child. He often brought toys and his mother's cinnamon rolls to those he visited at the hospital. He patiently visited angry children and teenagers like he'd once been until they opened up to him, and he talked about what it was like to have a prosthesis to other children who were facing amputation.

I could also count on John to visit and support teens who were dying. Knowing that a relapse could just as easily happen to them, most of the other teenagers found it too hard to cope with watching their friends die. John had the same fears and grief, but he still hung in there with his dying friends.

John and Eddie Greenhill became especially close, and after one of Eddie's relapses when he was admitted to the hospital for brain surgery, his mother recalled John pacing the hallways like an expectant father. For six hours, John got up and sat down, walked back and forth, and continuously stared at the doors of the surgery room. When Eddie was wheeled out of surgery, John followed his stretcher into intensive care. She said it was like he was with a fellow warrior.

In the following days, when Eddie woke up in a daze, he'd see John sitting in a chair next to his bed. Eddie told me, "Sometimes he was raiding my food, but most of the time he was just staring at me. It made me feel good that he was there."

Eddie considered John one of his best friends. Tellingly, both young men admitted that, in their pre-cancerous days, they would never have been friends.

John also assisted me with program planning for support groups and special events, and I trusted him implicitly. He attended college at Creighton University on a scholarship, and I am happy to say this cancer survivor is now the manager of a restaurant and an avid weightlifting buff.

Shawn Mayo: survivor

"This might sound strange, but I wouldn't change having cancer because it has made me a better person."

Shawn was a blond, pale-skinned sixteen-year-old who was diagnosed with leukemia in 1990. I had at least weekly contact with her for three years. Prior to being diagnosed, Shawn had diabetes, and the combination resulted in the sudden loss of her eyesight. Due to these combined medical problems, Shawn had to endure chemotherapy, multiple surgeries on her eyes, and major adjustments in her educational and social life. An outstanding student, her life's goal had been to be a veterinarian. Because of her visual impairment, vet school became unrealistic, but Shawn was able to redirect her energies and pursue a career in psychology with a specialty in the medical field.

I did not see this as Shawn accepting "second best" but rather as a testament to the advances she made in her people skills and the depth of compassion she acquired due to her own personal experience and involvement with other children and teens in treatment.

When Shawn first began chemotherapy and lost her vision, despite what appeared to be impossible hurdles, she continued to attend school and plan her future. We were all amazed at her strength, resiliency, and determination. She would always pick herself up, brush herself off, wipe away her tears, and say with a smile, "I can do it!" Shawn made most of these achievements independently. Her mother was divorced and struggling to support three children and wasn't always able to be with Shawn during her treatments.

When Shawn was first diagnosed and we were considering discharging her from the hospital, we said she had to have a nurse at home while her mother worked because she needed several blood tests and shots throughout the day.

Shawn, in a weakened condition and having gone from having good eyesight to being legally blind within a month, said she could handle her care herself. We didn't believe her for a moment but told her that if she could prove to the home care nurse that she could handle her medical and physical care safely, we would discontinue the use of a nursing assistant.

In two days, the nurse was gone.

Despite our advice to drop out of school for a while or to take only a few light courses, Shawn continued to take a full load of difficult courses. Again, she did the impossible.

Shawn won another battle when the state division of rehabilitation decided she should go to a college more adapted to the visually impaired than to the college of her choice. Without any family or financial assistance, she prepared her appeal and won the hearing.

Regarding community service and leadership, Shawn became one of the most outstanding members of our teen support group. She was always willing to meet and support new teens in treatment, and she made a significant difference in the emotional adjustment of several teens.

One teenage girl, Kym, who was treated at an adult hospital, came to SLCH every Thursday, Shawn's treatment day, to meet with Shawn for the emotional support she didn't receive at her own hospital. Both girls had a year's delay starting college due to their treatment, and this gave them a special bond.

Shawn wasn't very open about her feelings until she started sharing with Kym. One of the things neither teen liked was having those who didn't have cancer say to them, "I know how you feel." These friends *didn't* know how they felt. They also said friends tried to say things to make it better, but they couldn't. Shawn stated, "Everyone flocked around me when I was first diagnosed, then they all went off to college and I was left alone." She also noted that her friends were afraid to share the things they were doing because of all she was going through. This disconnect made Kym's friendship even more precious.

Both Shawn and Kym eventually learned to put things in better perspective. Neither wanted to dwell on dying. They saw other friends relapse two to three times, and while they struggled to accept this, they knew that if they personally relapsed, they would just have to go through it like others did.

Like some of my other favorite teens, Shawn became an official hospital volunteer and helped me organize several teen events. She was also a volunteer camp counselor at several camps for children with cancer. Shawn said that even though she liked to laugh and have fun, cancer made her a more serious and mature person. She stated, "This might sound strange, but I wouldn't change having cancer because it has made me a better person. I now open up more to others, and I also want to go out and help other people."

I'm happy to report that Shawn is now married and works in private consulting in Iowa. She was the executive director of BLIND, Inc. and is past president of the National Association of Blind Students (NABS). She oversaw the creation of Code Master, the most modern Braille learning system in the country, and was the recipient of the 2008 Bolotin Award on behalf of BLIND along with the directors of their other two national training centers. Her accomplishments are too numerous to list, and I am very proud of her and amazed at her achievements.

Marc Varady: 1969–1986

"Only a person who takes risks is free."

In February of 1986, at age sixteen, Marc was diagnosed with rhabdomyosarcoma of the testicle that had metastasized to the lymph nodes and lungs. Despite extensive surgeries, radiation, and very challenging chemotherapy, Mark became an integral part of our teen group in the short seven months he lived from his diagnosis to his death.

Besides our teen support group at the hospital, Marc was able to maintain his pre-cancer friendships, something that isn't always possible for teens. Perhaps part of the reason was the brevity of the time between diagnosis and death, but his personality probably also contributed.

And Then There Were Nine

Besides being intelligent, Marc had a great sense of humor, a ready smile, and the courage to be different. As one of his best friends said, "Marc had a love affair with life." He wasn't ashamed to go around bald, wear funny costumes, or talk about his cancer. He wrote in one friend's yearbook, "I'll see you next year, unless I die like everyone thinks I'm going to. Ha, Ha, Ha."

In the clinic, Marc always looked after the younger patients. He worked on our CURE pediatric cancer non-profit organization fundraisers and lightened everyone's life in the hospital with his sense of humor and wonderful spirit. As Michael Bradley, the parent of a young child with cancer who was president of our CURE board, wrote, "Marc could have been angry and bitter, but instead he was positive and compassionate. He could have been reclusive and self-absorbed, but instead he was open and caring."

The poem on the following page was found in Marc's wallet after his death. Versions of this poem have been attributed to William Arthur Ward, Leo Buscaglia, and Garett Polanco; the version Marc carried was from an anonymous author.

The Dilemma

To laugh is to risk appearing a fool.

To weep is to risk
appearing sentimental.

To reach out for another
is to risk involvement.

To expose feelings is to risk rejection.

To place your dreams
before the crowd is to risk ridicule.

To love is to risk
not being loved in return.

To go forward in the face of
overwhelming odds is to risk failure.

But risk must be taken because the
greatest hazard in life is to risk nothing.

The person who risks nothing, does
nothing, has nothing, is nothing.

He may avoid suffering and sorrow,
but he cannot learn, feel,
change, grow, or love.

Chained by his certitudes, he is a slave.

He has forfeited his freedom.

Only a person who takes risks is free.

Goldie Smith: 1973–2013

"She would be vomiting blood one day, then coming to the support group the next."

When she was fifteen years old, Goldie thought she had the flu until she was diagnosed with stage three Hodgkin's disease that required chemotherapy and radiation treatment to her lungs.

Not too many people look prettier without hair than with, but Goldie was one of them. She had caramel-colored skin, beautiful white teeth, and big brown eyes, and she liked to wear large hoop earrings. On days she was tired of her regal bald look, Goldie designed a hat to wear with curly black hair that looked very natural.

Goldie's personal connections at SLCH became very important to her, not only during treatment but long afterwards. The teen support group and the teen trip to Florida were probably more significant to her than to almost anyone else in the group. She would be vomiting blood one day, then coming to the support group the next. Goldie was very devoted to her friends in the teen group and made frequent visits to the hospital to visit others even on days she didn't have to be there.

Goldie said at first she thought she would die. She prayed her cancer would be cured, but she stated, "If not, I now know I made it through it once, and I can go through it many more times if I have to." Goldie's strength, like others in the teen group, came in part from seeing the examples of strength and coping her relapsed friends exhibited. Because she saw some of her friends die, she became wise beyond her years.

Goldie liked to call me her "other mother" and stayed in touch with me through cards, phone calls, and during our visits to St. Louis for the nineteen years after I left SLCH until she died from post-radiation therapy lung complications in May of 2013 at age thirty-nine. She always filled me in on how some of the other survivors were doing and on her own rich personal life. Despite the years of complications that compromised her respiratory system and gave her many bouts of dramatic edema that caused her body to swell up with fluid, Goldie always kept her sense of humor and had me laughing on the phone.

After her death, Al and I went to St. Louis for her visitation and spent time with her relatives, including her sisters and her four wonderful children, Marlana, Demetria (NiNi), Caleb, and Tylan. Although her life was cut short by the complications from radiation, her treatment gave Goldie many years of life that otherwise likely would have been stolen from her. Goldie knew she probably wouldn't live much longer as her complications increased, so my beautiful "daughter" always remembered to tell me how much she loved me before we hung up the phone.

Todd Wright: 1972–2013

"I don't think we realized that Todd came with an expiration date. I'm glad we didn't know it at the time or we might have missed some of the joy of his living."

Todd was eighteen and in his freshman year of college when he was diagnosed with leukemia. He was a very mature looking young man who already looked like he could be a financial broker. When Todd was in clinic one day, watching the little children in treatment playing, he told his mother, Jane, that he almost envied the little ones because they had no concept of the direness of their situation.

At first, Todd did not want to join what he called the "Cancer Club." He just wanted to be a normal person, but after his relapse, he found it helpful to be involved, and he quickly connected with the other teens.

Todd was known for his keen sense of humor. One day while he was hospitalized, a friend brought him ice cream packed in dry ice. Todd put the dry ice in his plastic bedside urinal, then called for his male nurse, Joe, to see the smoke pouring from it. He asked Joe, "What have you done to me?" and Joe was flummoxed until he caught on to the trick.

Todd came from an affluent family and was a classic example of how specific situations can create strange bedfellows. Although he was close to Shawn and Kris, whom I'll talk about later, he also became friends with Goldie, Eddie, John, and several others who would not have been his friends under different life circumstances.

In the time I was involved with Todd, he dealt with his initial treatment, a relapse, a bone marrow transplant at City of Hope Hospital in California, and many post-transplant issues, especially graft-versus-host disease (GVHD) complications. Todd's mother was his key support person for many years. Later, Jane told me she hadn't realized what it meant to Todd that she stayed with him through his arduous bone marrow transplant. Whenever she left his room to run an errand, he always asked how long she was going to be gone.

Years later, he told her how much it meant to him to have her there. This was true even when he was in his twenties. He figured that when she was out of the room, he had to be responsible for keeping himself alive, but when she came back, he could rest knowing she would take over that incredible responsibility. The last time Al and I saw Todd, he was in Barnes Hospital having aged out of SLCH. He said to me, "I'm not afraid to die. I just worry about how my death will impact my family and friends."

Although he had lingering side effects, especially a stooped posture from severe bone damage from all the years of chemotherapy and radiation treatment plus GVHD, Todd cheated death for years, met the love of his life, and became the father of twins in 2009. He had moved to Texas and become an investor. He also became a man of deep faith before the mysterious killer caught up with him in the form of another type of cancer in 2012. Although Todd hated leaving the people he loved, especially Jenna and their three-and-a-half-year-old twins, he was not afraid of dying and knew he would go to heaven. Todd died peacefully in January of 2013 at age thirty-nine with his wife and family members by his side. The family wrote, "Todd fearlessly faced death with clarity, composure, and a hearty dose of humor."

After his death, Jane said, "I don't think we realized that Todd came with an expiration date. I'm glad we didn't know it at the time or we might have missed some of the joy of his living."

One night about nine months after Todd's passing, Jane had what she called an "experience" rather than a dream. She said it was very brief but very real. She was standing up and hugging Todd and thinking, "You are tall again. You are strong again."

She could actually feel the strength of his arms around her and the muscles of his back through her arms around him. He was wearing white, and when she inhaled, she smelled his scent.

Although she was not particularly religious, this experience gave Jane comfort. She felt it was Todd's way of letting her know he was okay and that he was in Heaven.

Given all that the teenagers went through emotionally and physically during treatment, it's hard to explain why I found them to be such a joy. Yes, they sometimes shed tears and felt angry at their treatment and even at the system, but more often than not they laughed and engaged in genuine, heartfelt conversations.

My ability to connect them with each other and to create group programs for them was a far greater achievement than developing personal relationships with them. These teens came into the hospital angry, scared, and isolated. Helping them break through these emotions and seeing the bonds they created with each other always gave me a warm glow. I marveled at what kind, compassionate warriors they all became.

The next chapter is an example of my craziest idea and greatest feat. As you will see, it took an army of volunteers, most notably our son Tad, to get this idea off the ground.

Teen Trip to Florida

It's not unusual for a group of teenagers to take a trip to Florida during spring break, but for our teens in treatment for cancer, such a trip was only a dream. Nonetheless, every time we held a teen meeting and I asked what we should do next, someone would say, "Let's visit Tad and Gina in Florida!"

My twenty-six-year-old son, Tad, and his wife, Gina, had often volunteered at the hospital prior to moving to Sarasota, Florida. All the teens idolized them, not only because they were so nice but because they were both fitness champions.

I talked to Operation Liftoff, a non-profit organization that provides free flights for children, and though we didn't fit their criteria, they offered tickets donated by TWA employees for our "dream trip."

Fortunately, I did not estimate the work and cost of such a trip. Having faith in Tad, I just called to see what he could do to help, not appreciating that I was asking for the impossible since the trip would take place in April during Sarasota's prime tourist season and Tad was new to the area.

After making numerous phone calls that didn't pan out, Tad canceled his appointments and spent several days walking the beach on Longboat Key, personally visiting each place of business to explain our trip and request donations. Before he was through, he had secured everything we needed including condos, motels, meals at restaurants, vans, boat rides, a private ski show, carriage rides, snorkel gear, bicycles, T-shirts, and even pagers for staff. Gina pitched in and arranged a picnic on the beach sponsored by the physical therapy department of Doctors Hospital where she worked plus a special breakfast, gifts, and a welcoming speech from the mayor of Sarasota.

Once the ball of kindness started rolling, there was no stopping it. The parents of one teen who could not go secured tickets to Busch Gardens in Tampa donated by Anheuser-Busch. Dan Lehr, our hospital media man, volunteered to come on the trip and arranged video equipment so he could make souvenir tapes for each teen. Our teens raffled off items donated by parents and the St. Louis Blues hockey team to raise the extra money we still needed.

Behind the scenes, we busily worked out the details of each teen's treatment, making emergency backup plans we could implement in Florida, packing sunscreen lotions along with chemotherapy drugs, and planning for oxygen and wheelchairs. The day before the trip, we had a "teen tank-up" day in the clinic where we served hot dogs and popcorn along with blood and platelets. The excitement reverberated off the walls in the IV room.

With each special trip or camp I helped coordinate, I always sweated the details and reminded myself that, despite the best of plans, some patients would have to cancel at the last minute for medical reasons. This time, I had to add to my anxiety the absurdity of attempting to fly twenty-six teens with cancer and another seven support people, thirty-three in all, on standby due to the type of tickets that had been donated! I made backup plans B, C, and D, but, good luck, good people, and God were with us. Despite many tenuous medical situations, all twenty-six teens made it, and all thirty-three of us boarded the same flight!

Thanks to the TWA employees, we were treated like first-class passengers. The pilot's wife even baked cookies for us. During the trip, one passenger donated fifty dollars to the group, and another handed us a hundred-dollar bill. Such generosity continued to warm our hearts throughout our five days in Florida in April of 1992.

Despite some terminally ill teens, wheelchairs were often left in the corner of a condo, and our most serious medical problems were treating sunburns. We laughed a lot, slept very little, danced in the sun, and relished the many special activities and events put on just for us.

Carrie with her arms up in the air while riding on the back of one of the skiers

I'll never forget sitting in the stands for a private water ski show that Gina participated in. Fourteen-year-old Carrie, who had relapsed from a brain tumor and wasn't expected to live much longer, volunteered to ride on the back of one of the skiers. When she flashed past the stands with her arms up in the air, a look of sheer joy on her face, we all screamed with delight, tears running down our faces. Tad played music over the loudspeaker, and when the song "I'm Too Sexy" blared out, the teens who could started dancing in the bleachers while those who could not twirled their shirts, head scarves, and wigs.

Al and I still smile when we hear that song.

One evening at sunset, a few teens were out wading in the ocean when I told them this was the time of day when sharks fed. Eddie Greenhill told one of his friends that if he saw a shark, he should jump on his back and Eddie would just stand on his artificial leg, which would give the shark quite a surprise.

John sheds his leg for a swim

The last night, several of the older teens bundled up in blankets on the beach for most of the night. They were like a fortress trying to protect themselves and each other from the difficult months ahead. While they shared and laughed and attempted to ward off the harsh world of cancer, the night security guard on the beach, moved by their stories, helped keep watch over them. Al and I sat on lounge chairs nearby along with the medical staff. We kept a respectable distance so the teens could have their privacy.

Later, when we were alone, Corey Peterson told me about some of the discussions that went on under those blankets. Among the thoughts he shared with his friends and then with me were these: "We have grown up together. We have seen too much and lived through too much. The coping skills we used when we were younger as newly diagnosed thirteen- and fourteen-year-olds, primarily denial, won't work now that we're eighteen and nineteen. Now we have to stare death in the face, deal with it, and figure out how we can go on to live as best we can in the time we have left, whether that's six months or sixty years."

Tad holding teen on his shoulder

By the middle of the night, Corey was too tired to stay on the beach anymore, but he hated going in, so I went with him.

He told me, "I told Kris [Sellberg] we had to stay alive for each other." Choking up, he said, "I love Kris so much!" He then added, "You know I don't go to funerals, Jan, but I would go to Kris's, John's, Goldie's, and Todd's."

Kris had relapsed shortly before we left for Florida, so she knew this trip might be the last fun thing she lived to do. She'd had to battle and bargain with the medical staff to get permission to go, and I enjoyed watching her interact with all her friends. While sitting in the condo one day with Corey and Todd Wright, I heard Todd tell her, "I've got a great view." Her reply was, "Don't just lie there; get up and go get *in* your view!" While they talked, Corey fell asleep, and I watched Kris give him a gentle kiss on the forehead.

Two months after our return, we held a CURE teen reunion. We shared pictures, ate snacks, and watched the two-hour video our media man, Dan, had made on the big screen in the hospital auditorium. By then, one teen had died, two had relapsed, another had gone to Boston for experimental chemotherapy and surgery, one had been admitted to the bone marrow transplant unit, one was sleeping most of the time due to a brain tumor, and several were dealing with complications of chemotherapy.

At the reunion, Todd said, "We are only teens on the outside. Our bodies have betrayed us, and our minds have matured far beyond our other friends'. Ours is a special world. Our bond is a special bond."

With cancer, health and survival are not as predictable as the statistics would lead you to believe. The teenager most at risk of imminent death on this trip, Kris Sellberg, survived, yet several of her friends, including Corey, did not. Kris is now a cardiologist in Phoenix. She married and is the mother of three beautiful blond-haired children.

I often recall what one of the teens, Wendell, said on our way to the airport for this trip: "Half the battle is the cancer, and the other half is thinking about it." This spring break trip to Florida was my gift of love and Tad's gift of love to our teens whom I had known and loved for so long. I had no power or skill to cure them, but in my ten years at St. Louis Children's Hospital, I did everything I could to help them work on "the other half" of the battle. Whether they won or lost, I knew that someday we would dance together in the sun again.

In the complicated tapestry of this trip, a tug on any given thread could have unraveled the entire thing. What seemed impossible became possible. As the poem found in Marc Varady's wallet stated, to go forward in the face of overwhelming odds is to risk failure, but risk must be taken because the greatest hazard in life is to risk nothing.

Tips and Insights from the Teens

*I*n both our formal and informal sharing sessions, the teens in treatment had no problem expressing themselves. Topics ranged from parents to appearances to school, and what follows are some of their thoughts on what would have been helpful to hear from medical staff and others as well as what they found irritating and unhelpful.

On What to Say and What Not to Say

All the teens agreed they wanted to know "how bad it's going to be." More specifically, they wanted to know how bad the side effects of treatment would be, from pain and nausea to the impact on their social lives.

A strong consensus was that they hated having the reality of their treatment minimized. When this happened, they couldn't properly prepare for it, and they also felt that minimizing the impact of treatment discounted their suffering.

They also agreed that as much as they wanted to be honestly informed about treatment side effects, they did not want to know the statistics on their chances of survival unless their chances were very good.

Classic offensive statements from medical staff included the following:

- *"There will be a little discomfort."* The teens wanted pain called what it was—pain! In addition, they resented being made to feel "like a baby" for being upset about it.
- *"You'll just feel a little pressure."* Again, the teens were offended by having their pain minimized. One teen said about a bone marrow aspirate, "It felt like I was being shot. I've never been shot, but that must be what it feels like!"
- *"You might have a little nausea."* According to the teens, this meant they were going to throw their guts up.
- *"You'll be able to lead a normal social life."* This wasn't true, declared the teens. Treatment did interfere with their social lives. Often, special events ended up being held on treatment day or shortly thereafter when they were too sick to care. In addition, low blood counts often meant they couldn't attend basketball games, school events, and the like.

The teens also objected to staff being "too cheerful" when they were sick and hospitalized or at the clinic for treatment. One teen mockingly imitated, "Oh, isn't it a beautiful day! I'll bet you wish you were outside!"

Another teen said, "The staff only see you a few times a month if you're an outpatient. At the end of the day, they get to go home and go on with their lives. They don't realize the hour-to-hour impact treatment has on our lives. They can afford to be cheerful!"

Another big issue involved window shades. Staff became concerned when the rooms of hospitalized teens were dark all day, but the teens resented having someone insist the shades be open for their mental health. The consensus was, "I *like* the shades closed" and "I *like* living in the dark!"

A few teens added that when they were receiving chemotherapy, their eyes were sensitive to the light, and most said they kept their bedrooms dark at home. One teen even said his room at home was called "The Cave."

It especially bothered the teens to have someone come into their rooms when they were sleeping and open the shades. It was just another indication of how little control they had.

On Parents

Teens often discussed the challenges of dealing with overprotective parents. One of the biggest issues was parents nagging them to eat. One teen explained, "I don't only have to think about how the food is going to taste going down but how it's going to taste coming back up!"

Most resented being kept from social activities due to a parent's concern, but a few teens mentioned that they felt their parents pushed them too much to be socially active and to act cheerful.

We agreed that their parents probably needed them to act as if they were doing better than they were in order for the parents themselves to feel better.

On Appearances

From hair loss due to chemotherapy to the "fat face" teens on steroids developed, being treated for cancer did a number on how they looked.

The group agreed that hair loss was generally more difficult for girls yet having broviacs—central lines inserted into the body for long-term access that hung out and were capped and taped on—was more of an issue for boys. Since boys often went shirtless, they couldn't hide broviacs. The lines also interfered with sports, meant kids couldn't swim, and made the teens, in their words, "look sickly."

All the teens hated appearing sickly and went to great lengths in order to look tougher than they felt. One teen summed it up this way: "Just when I was feeling my weakest, I had to act my toughest."

During my ten years at the hospital, port-a-caths, which were entirely under the skin, became an option. The teens said they involved more pain because the needle had to pierce the skin, but otherwise port-a-caths were preferable to broviacs because they weren't as unsightly, the teens didn't to have to take as many precautions, and port-a-caths didn't have to be irrigated daily.

On the other hand, one teen said the bump left under the skin "looked like Mount Everest."

This was an exaggeration, but it was still obvious a device was under the skin, and the teens hated this.

On School

Some of the teens struggled with teachers who weren't flexible about makeup work. Either I contacted the schools about this issue or a volunteer who specialized in working with schools did. Teens hated feeling apprehensive and overwhelmed by make-up work, which made going through treatment "a double whammy."

The more overwhelmed the teens felt, the more reluctant they were to attend school. This was a problem for many reasons, including the fact that socialization is so important for teens but especially for those teens who are undergoing treatment.

How much of an issue socialization became mostly depended on how outgoing the teens were and how open they were to talking about their illness. The quieter adolescents had more isolation, and sometimes more ridicule, to deal with.

Tips and Insights from the Teens

On Fighting Treatment

Most of the teens said they ended up fighting with their parents about going in for treatment, and one girl in our group told how she locked herself in the bedroom the last time she was to come in.

I said that perhaps teenagers were old enough to make their own decisions in this regard. Then I asked how they would feel if their parents left the choice entirely up to them. I said, "What if your parents said, 'If you don't want to go for treatment, that's fine with me'"? Then I reminded the teens that they would probably die without treatment but perhaps that was also their choice.

There was stunned silence for a moment, then one teen said, "I would think my mom had gone crazy if she said that!"

We concluded that the teens understandably hated going in for treatment and needed someone to be angry at. Who better to act out against than your parents, who, for your own good, will make you go anyway?

Teens are challenging under the best of circumstances. Raising teens who are undergoing treatment for life-threatening diseases quadruples the challenge. Typically, parents try their best to do what's right by their teenagers, but when their child is being treated for a life-threatening condition, sometimes their best is not enough. That's why it's so important to have the right medical staff and the right support services.

Though it was sometimes brutal, I absolutely loved the teens' honesty. I learned more from them than from any professional course I could have taken. This was also true for other staff as long as they weren't condescending and willingly listened to what the teens had to say rather than told them what they should be thinking and feeling.

Beyond the Child with Cancer

*H*aving a child with cancer forever changes the family. Everyone is impacted, from parents to siblings to extended family members.

If you're a parent, you leave the world of normalcy the day your child is diagnosed. From here on out, your every thought and action revolves around the child in treatment. Needless to say, you no longer know how to engage in social chitchat. When someone starts talking about remodeling their kitchen or their recent cruise to the Bahamas, you want to shout, "Who cares!" When they complain about their child getting a D in math, you get angry that they don't appreciate the fact that their child is alive and healthy. You become tearful when you get an invitation to a graduation or wedding because you know your child might never live to celebrate such events.

You don't want to be isolated, but you know it's not easy to be your friend right now. Friends and relatives tend to tiptoe around you because they don't know what might be hurtful or helpful to say, and you sometimes don't know yourself.

You fear every cough might be pneumonia and every fever might be an infection. You're afraid that if you aren't constantly vigilant, staff or a visitor might come in without washing their hands, might fail to cover their mouths and noses with a mask when they cough or sneeze, might have an undiagnosed virus. You're afraid your child won't get the right medicine at the right time. You're afraid a resident will come in who doesn't know your child and will make decisions based on a lack of history. You're afraid an IV will be put in improperly and medication will infiltrate. The list goes on and on. You're afraid of many things, and you need support.

My husband calls me "the queen of support groups." I've always felt that a group of people going through similar experiences can help each other more than a paid professional can help them, so I set up support groups for teens with cancer, support groups for siblings, bereavement support groups, Prader-Willi syndrome support groups, and of course support groups for parents.

Parents of children with cancer often share common challenges. Chief among them is cancer's detrimental impact on intimacy. Keeping intimacy a priority in the marriage can be the best thing you can do for your child on treatment, for your other children, and for yourself, but when cancer strikes, relationships often fall to the bottom of the list of priorities. As one parent said, "Sometimes marriages are reduced to sex and good manners, and when you have a child in treatment, sometimes it's reduced to just good manners!"

Couples in crisis desire closeness, but there are many obstacles in their way, including a lack of time. Parents are often like relay runners, connecting just briefly enough to pass the torch—typically child care instructions and car keys—to their spouses. Many parents feel a sense of hopelessness about the marriage or a sense of guilt if they desire intimacy. They typically feel it's wrong to indulge their own needs and pleasures when their child is so critically ill.

Even if they don't feel guilty, the sheer logistics of finding intimate time often takes more energy and creativity than parents can muster up. Like one parent in the group said, "Desperate sex is rendezvousing in the van in the hospital parking lot."

The problem with putting your marriage on hold is that children with cancer are living longer. Certainly, living longer isn't the problem. The problem is that treatment is more complex and often consumes many months and years of priority attention. During this time, making continuous critical medical decisions creates additional stress. As one parent said, "I have to live with my decisions about our child's treatment the rest of my life. I don't have to live with you!"

Often, one parent assumes the emotional and physical burden of becoming the medical expert and the other doesn't share this responsibility, which leads to resentment in both parties. The same asymmetry becomes stressful if one parent deals more openly than the other with the fear their child is going to die. The reflection "You don't have to feel what I feel but you have to listen to how I feel" should be taped on the bedroom mirror of parents whose child is diagnosed with cancer.

Even if your spouse doesn't share your beliefs and fears, it's crucial to validate each other's feelings. If this doesn't happen, the sense of separateness spreads and couples begin to avoid talking about substantive things. Watching TV might feel safer than talking, but there's nothing lonelier than feeling alone when you're together.

In a "Mothers Only" group, the two most common problematic issues the moms discussed were a lack of alone time with their spouses and a lack of communication. Not surprisingly, these two issues created multiple side effects.

The mothers felt they had lost the ability to be happy, fun-loving partners. They no longer felt sensual and had no emotional or physical energy left for their husbands. Communication with their spouses always seemed focused on their child and the illness.

At the same time, their husbands generally avoided or rejected their efforts to communicate their feelings.

In addition, men and women often had a different emotional response to the illness and to life in general. Husbands often had more opportunity to escape through work or sports. By contrast, several mothers quit their jobs to care for their sick child. Overall, most felt they had become the "super responsible" parent.

It's critical for parents whose children are fighting cancer to know that their marriage does not have to self-destruct. So much is out of your control when your child is being treated for cancer that it's important to know there is one thing you can still control by doing some preventative work—your marriage. The illness can even be a catalyst for positive change if couples are aware of the pitfalls and work together to avoid them. I always counsel parents not to let one tragedy multiply into others, but parents aren't the only ones impacted by a child's diagnosis of cancer—siblings are deeply challenged too.

Kati was thirteen when her twelve-year-old sister, Julie, died in May of 1982 after a seven-year struggle with cancer. The girls' parents had divorced shortly before Julie was diagnosed, and the girls were being raised alone by their mother. Kati was very sick shortly after the divorce, their mom was isolated in an old farmhouse with the two girls, and then, during a routine tonsillectomy, Julie's cancer was discovered.

Six months after Julie's death, Kati reflected on the difficulty of those years and on how much she misses her sister.

Sibling Kati's Story

Mom got a little crazy during the time of the divorce, crying and hollering. I don't remember much except that she cried when Dad left and told me he had a sickness in his head. I don't think I was afraid or upset, yet I kept getting very sick and vomiting and running a high fever. The doctors never did find anything wrong with me. They think it might have been due to the divorce. We also wondered if that didn't start Julie's cancer. It started in her chest. She had a really awful kind, but they did surgery and thought she was going to be okay. I always thought she was going to be okay. To me, Julie was always "getting better"—until the day she died.

I never expected her to die. They said she was going to die many times, yet she would get better, so I never really believed them. Whenever things got bad, I would say, "God will take care of it!" And whenever anything went right or Julie would get a little better, I would say, "See, he did!"

When Julie died, I guess I was in shock. I really didn't feel much of anything. I know I didn't believe she was dead. I kept thinking, "She'll wake up…Now cut it out, Julie, and get up!"

Julie had three operations. Everything looked okay for a while, then she fell and hurt her head. She had a huge bump and my mom wanted it x-rayed, but the doctor kept saying, "It's just a bump, I know!" Mom responded, "She's my kid, and I know!" He finally agreed to x-ray it, but meanwhile some time went by. The x-ray showed there was cancer in her head, chest, and other places. After that, Mom changed to Dr. O'Connor. He was always great with Julie.

Mom lost her brother to Hodgkin's disease when she was sixteen so she knows some of what I've gone through, but she says she knows it's not the same since Julie and I were so close. I used to watch her after school and whenever Mom had to go somewhere.

I never resented Julie for taking so much of Mom's time and attention, but I did resent Mom for giving Julie special privileges. She let her buy heels and wear make-up at a much younger age than I got to. It seems silly, but that was a big deal for me. Now I'm glad she did, because otherwise Julie wouldn't have had a chance to do those things.

My friends didn't understand why I couldn't go places with them or wasn't as much fun as I used to be. They all lived in safe little worlds where their biggest concern was what dress to buy or that their moms didn't understand them. At the time, keeping Julie out of pain was my mom's and my life. We tried so hard and sometimes stayed up all night, but Julie would still scream and cry out in pain.

Julie ended up with bone cancer, the most painful kind. We tried so hard, but the last six months, I couldn't even get her to smile. Once I got so angry that I hollered, "Dammit, Julie! Why can't you just smile for once?" She put a fake smile on her face and just stared at me.

Even the school counselor couldn't understand. He called me in to talk one day because he'd found out my parents were divorced, my dad had problems, and my sister was dying. I think he felt bad that I never went back to talk to him, but I didn't think he could help. He just talked the whole time and didn't really ask anything about me. He assumed he knew what was going on with me and let me know how many kids came to see him.

It would have been helpful if my friends had let me talk. They always asked how Julie was doing but didn't really want to hear about it. Also, it would have helped if they'd understood why I couldn't go places with them, that I really needed to be with Julie. They always pushed me, saying, "Well, why can't you go?" They acted angry at me. When Julie died, they backed away. I know they tried, but they didn't know what to say so they started avoiding me.

My relatives didn't know what to say or do either. My grandma always came over to "help," but this was really hard on us. She would complain about every little thing and sit down and tell Julie about her own aches and pains! Grandma always told us we didn't appreciate the help she gave us. Julie got to where she didn't want to see Grandma, so I would say she was sleeping.

My grandma didn't understand about Julie and me either. Like the time Grandma and I had to rush her to the hospital when Mom was at work. Julie was in so much pain that all she wanted to do was squeeze my hand. Grandma kept reaching her hand over. She thought Julie should want to hold her hand because she was the grandma. She just didn't understand.

Before Julie got really sick, when Mom would go out, we would stay up late and watch TV and eat popcorn and talk. When I was upset with Mom or Grandma, I could talk to Julie about it. She understood because she felt the same way a lot. Julie would share gifts with me that other people brought to her, and she "willed" me her bed.

I miss her a lot. Sometimes I'm okay, but when I see some of the things she wrote to me or remember something we did, I start crying. I try not to let people know I still get upset. They think that since it's been almost six months since Julie died, I should be better by now.

I would talk to her in my head right after she died like she was still there. My mom has a king-size waterbed, and Julie often slept on one side. Now that we're redoing my bedroom, I sleep with my mom. At first I didn't want to sleep on "Julie's side," but now I do, and I can really feel her presence.

That last night, we worked so hard to keep her alive. All night long we put hot packs on her. We were so busy that I didn't think about her dying. After she died, we stayed with her for three hours. It felt good to do that, and I talked to her and told her all the things I wanted to tell her. I'm glad I was with her when she died.

I know this will sound silly, but my mom asked our neighbor to wash Julie after she died, and I was hurt. I wish she had asked me. I know that sounds weird, but for some reason, it was important to me.

I talked to Kati about the fact that, out of need, she had pretty much taken on the role of an adult along with her mother because her help was so needed and because her mom's energy had been directed at Julie. I said it must be a huge change for her and her mom now that there were just the two of them and she was now an only child. I told Kati it would be natural for her mom to get protective about her and want her to suddenly be a child again.

Kati responded, "You're right! That's *really* been hard! I was allowed to do pretty much what I wanted before. Mom was more like my sister. Now she worries about me more and doesn't want me to be alone. She feels guilty if she goes out and leaves me, but sometimes I like being alone. It's funny, but even though there's just two of us now, the house seems more crowded."

Kati added, "I have to admit that I also worry about her more. One night she didn't leave a note and I worried about her all evening. Since Julie died, I worry about Mom getting into an accident. The day after Julie died, Mom and I were in the car together, and I wished the car would roll over and we would die together.

"Now, though, I worry and dream about Mom dying. I really have nowhere to go that would be okay to live if she died."

Beyond the child who is afflicted, cancer impacts everyone in the family, changing roles and expectations in ways that can be difficult to accept, especially when these roles and expectations keep changing. Often, relationships need to be reestablished, including those with parents, siblings, spouses, and/or other children. It's also important to learn to forgive when parents, spouses, siblings, or other children are not as sensitive and understanding as you need them to be. You learn a lot about unconditional love when you go through the long trauma of having a child in the family undergo treatment for cancer.

It's Not Over When It's Over

*W*hat happens when children finish treatment and their cancer is in remission? A number of issues typically present themselves in this long-hoped-for time for children and parents both. These challenges usually come as a surprise and disappointment to the parents, children, and teens who expected life to go back to normal.

How Do I Get My Attention Now?

As awful as cancer treatment can be and as much as children of all ages can't wait until it's over, they often feel an unexpected void when treatment is complete. Teachers no longer make exceptions for them. No one asks how they're feeling or tells them how brave and wonderful they are. They no longer get out of school or receive special presents. They're now supposed to return to being "ordinary," but they don't feel ordinary

Shortly after a seven-year-old girl completed three years of chemotherapy, her mom called me in a state of shock to tell me her daughter had reported her for child abuse.

When I talked to this angelic-faced child with long blonde hair, she batted her baby blue eyes and told me she'd made up the story to get attention from her teacher and classmates in her new school who didn't know she'd had leukemia. She then admitted she got more attention at home than she'd bargained for!

How Do I Fit in and Keep Up?

Children and teenagers whose cancer is in remission typically feel they no longer fit in with their peers. The process matures them far beyond others their own age, so they often feel emotionally isolated. Frequently, life at school feels like it has gone on without them.

Those with physical changes such as a limb amputation, large scars, or hair that does not entirely grow back after radiation to the head find that the further out they are from treatment, the less protected they are from ridicule.

Chemotherapy and radiation to the head can create new learning challenges, but once the signs of treatment are no longer visible, teachers often discount the need for special educational and testing accommodations. Children can get frustrated when they can't keep up in class, and teenagers often worry that these new learning challenges will keep them from achieving their educational goals for college.

What Is Normal?

Parents attempting to sort out typical psychological development and/or normal medical symptoms in a child who has completed treatment often worry about both overreacting and underreacting.

Parents who've overreacted often get the dreaded, condescending tone from medical staff that begins with the statement, "Now, Mother…" Parents rightly interpret this to mean, "You're just another hysterical parent."

It's Not Over When It's Over

On the other hand, parents who let a symptom slide and finally go to the doctor might have to face a raised eyebrow and the statement, "So how long has he had these symptoms?" They rightly interpret this as meaning "You've been neglectful."

All kids get fevers. If your child had a fever when first diagnosed, your throat will get dry every time the thermometer reaches 99.5°. If your child is doing poorly in math, you will wonder if it's due to laziness or a learning disability caused by treatment. If your teenager tends to weep a lot, you'll wonder, do *all* thirteen-year-old girls cry so easily?

The answers are seldom black or white, so you sit and mull over the gray areas for hours or days before you swallow your pride, take a deep breath, and pick up the phone.

The Dreaded Checkups

When treatment begins, parents typically think the magic day when all their worries will subside will come shortly after the last treatment.

Why then do their hands sweat as they sit in suite D waiting for the routine checkup?

The problem with cancer is that it's so sneaky. The symptoms are often vague, common symptoms of many run-of-the-mill illnesses that both parents and their local pediatrician might discount. Therefore, the only reassurance comes after a thorough checkup from the hematology/oncology staff.

On the other hand, parents know that one visit in suite D can change their lives forever.

If you're like most parents, about a week before the big checkup, morbid thoughts will flash through your head that you try to block out. Finally, by the night before the checkup, you give up any pretense of getting a good night's sleep.

Of course, when you come to the clinic, everyone expects you to be jovial because your child is off treatment. You put on a fake smile and pretend you're reading a magazine while all the little bald-headed reminders of what has been, and what still could be, play around you.

Losing Your "Crutch"

As much as parents hate those weekly trips to the clinic for treatment and wonder why curing cancer has to be so barbaric, it's hard to trust doing nothing.

When treatment finally ended for one child whose regimen began at eight months of age, his mother said to me, only half joking, "Couldn't they just give him a little bit of chemotherapy for the rest of his life?"

When your child looks a little peaked, you would give anything to be able to run down to the hospital for a blood test so you can sleep better. Then, when you call the hematology/oncology office and hear, "Why don't you just take him to your local pediatrician?" you realize your crutch has been knocked out from under you and you're going to have to learn to walk independently all over again.

Moving Back into Your Own Bed

When a child is first diagnosed, parents panic over every cough and moan. Naturally, many parents inadvertently get into the bad habit of sleeping in the same bedroom with their child. Of course, then a young sibling might feel left out and crawl into bed with the other parent.

About the time you and your spouse look longingly at each other and decide that "tonight's the night" to wean everyone back into their own beds, your child on treatment begins to run a low-grade fever. Naturally, you resolve that next week is the week. Besides, who has the energy for what sleeping in the same bed might lead to?

By the time treatment gets easier, or is complete, the emotional dependency problems are hard to break. What's more, by now, you and your spouse might be separated by more than a bedroom door.

Do We Still Like Each Other?

In many ways, our society sabotages "alone time" for parents. After-school activities, scouts, dancing lessons, baseball games, music lessons, school events, and endless household chores often keep parents running in separate directions. Add to this list chemotherapy treatments, post-chemotherapy symptoms, hospitalizations, resentful siblings demanding attention, and the need to go to work, and it's no wonder some parents barely remember each other's names.

During hospitalizations, you and your spouse often have a mere thirty minutes together a day during the "changing of the guards." In this time, you must relay essential information such as "Don't forget to..." while contending with the ongoing physical and emotional needs of your child and interruptions from staff.

By the time treatment is over, you might not even know if you want to spend time together. This person who once was your lover, confident, and dancing partner might now feel more like a business partner. It's time to ask yourselves a question: "Did we like each other before all this began?"

If the answer is yes, the next question is, "Is there still a relationship left to nurture?" Then, "Are we still willing to commit to the time needed to get to know each other again?"

So This Is "Happily Ever After"?

When your child was diagnosed, you thought you would probably go crazy.

Well, you didn't, or at least not crazy enough for most people to notice. You survived the seemingly unending months or years of treatment. The good times have arrived!

But if that's the case, why are the kids still fighting? Why is your spouse still complaining? Why is there still not enough money to go around? Worst of all, why does this child you were so terrified of losing act so obnoxiously at times that you don't even like being around him or her?

Once, when we were going through a crisis, my husband said to me, "Won't it be nice when we can start worrying about cleaning out our closets again?"

The problem is, the day does come when you start worrying about clean closets again along with other mundane things, but you don't necessarily feel as happy and relieved as you thought you would. This is normal. This is life.

When the nightmare of cancer begins, most parents pray, "Dear God, just get us through this and I'll never complain again about…" Although such a significant life crisis can change us in some positive ways, at some point our humanness creeps back in—in spite of ourselves.

My advice is, don't worry about it. Life is never going to be perfect, and God is used to people making bargains they can't keep. You and your partner and your children will be partly enriched and partly damaged by this experience. You can nurture the enriched part and minimize the damaged part by accepting yourself, your spouse, and your children with all the normal faults and feelings that accompany any family that deals with childhood cancer.

Poignant Final Days

As I mentioned earlier, my thoughts on what comes after death have vacillated. Because my work has exposed me to the unfairness of life, I can't help but hope there is an afterlife permeated by goodness and beauty and love.

This chapter highlights a few examples of final words from children I knew that offer the hope of something after death. Is it heaven as many of us envision it? I will let the words of these beautiful angels help you decide.

Jennifer, eight years old

When she learned her leukemia was back, Jennifer cried all the way home. She said, "But Mommy, I can't die—I have got my new puppy to raise. Who will train my puppy?"

After some boys made fun of her appearance, Jennifer, who was heavy from steroids and bald from chemotherapy, told her mom, "When I die, I'm going to be skinny, have long hair, and play with Aaron." Aaron was a friend who had died.

Towards the end, when she was sleeping most of the time, Jennifer asked her mom to make sure she was holding a piece of gum at all times. She wanted to give it to Aaron when she saw him in heaven because he loved gum. He used to send it to her in the transplant unit.

Jennifer was bleeding and in pain but coherent until the moment she died. She asked, "Oh Mom, why me?" One morning, she asked her mom to read her a book about heaven and to hold her. She asked, "Mommy, are you sure God is going to let me into heaven?"

Her mom said yes and continued reading to her from the Bible. Suddenly Jennifer said, "Mommy, Mommy, I see heaven!" At that moment, she died in her mother's arms.

I still don't fully know what I believe, but I *do* believe Aaron got his gum.

Corey, five years old

Corey was diagnosed with an aggressive leukemia in April of 1984 at the age of three. The only child of Carla and Mark, Corey had a great imagination. He like to watch the daytime soap opera *Days of Our Lives* and told me, "They do a lot of kissing there!"

Corey told me about his imaginary girlfriend and said that, when he was five, they were going to live together. He said she had brown hair, wore a blue shirt and red shorts, and had eyes just like his, but he didn't want to marry her because he didn't want to have to kiss the bride!

The day before Corey's death at home, I called his mom. At that point, Corey couldn't hear or see well.

She told me, "It feels like there's someone here between us because he keeps telling someone to get away from him and shouting, 'No! I love my mommy, not you!' Then he settles down and says, 'Okay, Okay.'"

The next morning, Cory asked his mom to hold him. He said, "Do you still love me?" and then died in her arms.

Carrie, two years old

Carrie had neuroblastoma, a very lethal form of cancer. A few days before she died, Carrie said, "I see ghosts. I see Daddy!" She had never seen her dad or mentioned him before. He had died three months before she was born.

Jason, four years old

For weeks, Jason said he was going to be okay. The morning he died, on his birthday, he said, "I'm not going to be okay anymore—I'm going to die today." He did.

Aaron, three years old

On his last day, although he had not been talking or moving much, Aaron suddenly said, "Momma, I can say my ABCs!" He then said, "I think I need to lie down because I see them coming for me." He then asked, "Can I go to sleep now? Momma, I love you," and then he died.

Ladonna, fifteen years old

Pink was LaDonna's favorite color. Just before she died, she said, "Mama, I'm dead, I'm dead! There ain't nothing here but pink and white. There ain't nothing dark here. Lord, take me home!" She then fell back on the bed and died.

Kyle, eighteen years old

Kyle was an only child, and his friends were exceptionally supportive of him during his illness and of his parents after his death.

One young couple came to sit with him rather than go out on a date. Every night, groups of friends came to see him after he was too sick to go out. A female friend away at college called every night. When Kyle became weaker, his mother would hold the phone to his ear so they could talk. The night Kyle became too weak to say clear sentences, his friend cried, and tears rolled down Kyle's cheeks.

His mother, Renee, told me that shortly before he died, Kyle said to her, "I never had a chance to be in love…Mom, you taught me everything there is to know. Teach me how to let go."

His mother responded, "I don't know how to, Kyle. I don't know how to let go of you."

Jason Struble: 1972–1992

*I*n February of 1990, seventeen-year-old Jason discovered he had testicular cancer with metastases to his abdomen and lungs. Jason could have appeared in chapter two with the other teens, but his thoughts on death were so eloquent that I decided to include his story here.

Although only one percent of all male malignancies are testicular cancer, it's the most common carcinoma in males between fifteen and thirty-five. If caught early enough, it has a high cure rate, but like many young men, Jason at first ignored the symptom of an enlarged testicle out of embarrassment. It was only after playing a basketball game when he became very breathless and felt pain in his chest that he said something to his parents.

Jason fought a courageous battle for two years and two months, enduring countless rounds of chemotherapy, a bone marrow transplant, and many surgeries. He died peacefully at home and in his sleep, just as he'd wished to do.

Jason shared many thoughts in the last weeks of his life, primarily with his mother, Doris, who then shared the thoughts and words of this amazing young man with me:

Is there basketball in heaven?

Did my life make a difference?

Am I a good kisser? I never kissed a girl.

I can't control what's happening to my body; I can only control my attitude.

Doesn't Dad know that I have to hear him say he loves me?

I hope you don't wear sandals in heaven; my feet are such a mess!

How will I know when to quit fighting?

If I ever did anything with Make-A-Wish or Dream Factory, I wouldn't take a trip or have a sport star visit; I'd ask Dr. Robert Schuller or Norman Vincent Peale to come visit me.

I want Dad to have my baseball hats. Dad, throw away all those farmer hats. You are not a farmer!

I want Coach Porter to have my basketball hoop and my weight bench and weights.

I guess you can give my clothes to Larry Rice for the inner city mission.

Jason also shared many thoughts about his sister, Jen:

I want Jen to work harder and get good grades. She would be a good vet. That has always been her dream. I want Jen to have my savings, Mom, but you monitor the funds so they only get used for important things.

After I die, will you please continue organizing my baseball cards and label all of them? Pack them neatly in boxes and put them in the attic. Maybe someday Jen will have kids and they will want something that belonged to their Uncle Jason.

I want you to buy Jen a heart-shaped locket. Put my picture inside and inscribe it, "Jen—I love you, Jason." Then, when she feels discouraged and wants to quit, she can look at the locket and think of me and work harder.

I feel so sorry for Jen. It must be hard for her. I cannot fathom how I would feel if she were dying.

Oh, Mom, I won't be here to take care of you when you're old. I must make Jen promise that she

will take good care of you when you're old.

Jason had much to say to his mom too:

I would not have lived this long, Mom, without your support and love. You are the reason I could fight for so long...

Mom, have them play "You Are the Wind beneath My Wings" at my funeral as a tribute from me to you because you are my inspiration...

Mom, what could I ever give you to repay you for all you have done for me or show you how much I love you? You ought to go to the baseball game and sit in the bleachers with Chi-Chi after I die and have some fun. You haven't had any fun in the last two years. Mom, you are to go on a vacation after I die or on a cruise and relax.

Mom, you should have some kind of calling after I die. Do something to help others. I want you to go to all the junior high schools in St. Louis and tell the boys about testicular cancer.

Mom, when you go outside at night, find where the North Star is located and think of me.

Jason also reflected on death:

> *Mom, I can die now. I made peace with Dad and I feel ready. I think I'm going to die over the next three days because Jen is home. [Jason died two days later.]*
>
> *I feel so at peace...I am not afraid to die. I'm only afraid of how I will die. I hope it is in my sleep. Will I die of lung failure or heart failure?*
>
> *I wish I knew when I was going to die so you could be holding my hand, Mom. Being born and dying are easy. It's what's in between that's so hard...*
>
> *All in all, I've had a good life. My only regrets are that I did not play basketball my junior year in high school, I did not get to college, and I won't be a father—I would have been a good dad.*
>
> *All in all, I've had a good life.*

He also helped plan his funeral:

> *Now, Mom, this casket isn't one of those deals where you have to be sanding, staining, and polishing it, is it? [Jason had just learned his parents had picked an oak casket for him.]*
>
> *How will you invite people to my funeral? How will they know to come?*
>
> *I want a party after my funeral. In fact, it would be nice if you invited all the people over to the house afterwards to eat...I wish I was strong enough to have my funeral party before I died so I could tell everyone myself how much I love them.*

I don't want people to wear black to my funeral. I want bright, happy colors, and I want people to leave feeling good inside.

What should I wear in my casket? In the winter I might be cold! I want to wear a white tux when I'm buried with a bright bow tie. I never wore a tux. I want to have a boutonniere and you to wear a matching corsage.

Tell Dad not to wear any of those frumpy brown sports coats to my funeral.

I want them to rub my body with Skin So Soft so when you kiss me in the casket, like you did Grandma, I will smell good...

I want to be buried with the Bible, a picture of our family, and the prayer hanky I was given in the bone marrow transplant unit...I'm so lucky to be planning my own funeral. Not everybody gets to do that. Who would have believed I am having so much fun planning my funeral?

Jason died peacefully three hours later, pain free, at home, with his mom holding his hand.

As Jason had requested, his basketball coach, Dave Porter, spoke. Likewise, his mom delivered the eulogy at his celebration of life because, as Jason said, "You know me best." Balloons decorated the church and everyone wore bright colors. Afterwards, homemade cookies and lemonade were served. I like to picture Jason smiling down, thinking, "Well done!"

When I think about the children and teenagers and families I worked with and the grief they felt, the following words written by Miss Virginia Barckley resonate with me: "All grief must not be thought of as dreary and destructive. The world would be worse without it. If no man's life were significant enough to cause weeping, if birth and death were unmarked, if the measure of our years on earth were nothing, we might better be houseflies rather than human beings, made in God's image. Profound grief is preceded by deep love which gives life meaning. In the deepest sense, our days would be empty and futile if we never grieved, or, never dying, left emotional chaos behind us."

Lessons from a Bereaved Mom

*L*osing a child is something we don't even want to imagine, so most human beings do all they can to keep such horrible thoughts at bay.

I don't like envisioning this heartbreaking possibility either, but my work has taught me what a privilege it is to help people who are in the depths of despair find comfort and relief. This is why, in addition to organizing and leading bereavement groups for parents who have lost their children to cancer, other diseases, and accidents, I volunteered to be the counselor for the local homicide bereavement group in Sarasota, Florida, after leaving St. Louis Children's Hospital.

When I first began leading parent support groups at SLCH, I would come home with a stomachache from holding in so much sorrow. What helped the most was accepting there was nothing I could do to ease their pain except let them talk and share with each other. There were no magic words I could say to make it better.

Because there has been a lot written on grief, I do not spend much time on it in this book, but I want to share the following profound excerpts from a lengthy writing given to me by Susan Abbott that she turned into a booklet in 1994 after the death of her son. Diagnosed at age thirteen with the more life-threatening type of leukemia, acute myelogenous leukemia (AML), Jim died during the bone marrow transplant process.

Jim Abbott

Jim was very close to his mother. He did not have much time before his transplant to be very involved with our teen group, but he did attend the overnight slumber party for teens at our home the night Corey Peterson starred in the play *Ten Little Indians*. Afterwards, he said, "This is the best time I've had since I was diagnosed!"

Excerpts from Lessons by Susan Abbott

It's been a time of the re-examination of the very roots of existence and the very basics of belief—a time of questioning, of evaluating, of learning. And the learning is perhaps the most important tool—my own personal yardstick of comparison of where I've been and where

Lessons from a Bereaved Mom

I am—of figuring out just where this roller coaster of grief is taking me. And this is what I have discovered.

I have learned that I am stronger than I thought—that I can survive against the most devastating blow a person can sustain and though surviving is not the same as living, it is more than I expected. I have withstood a living hell, I have walked through fire, I have endured that which is beyond endurance, and I have kept on going. And though sometimes one step forward means two steps backwards, I know I will keep on going. For there is no hell, there is no fire— there is nothing that could come closer to destroying me than the loss of my son.

I have learned that I am much weaker than I knew—I am unable to help those closest to me; I cannot shoulder another's pain without breaking—without shattering—into pieces that cannot be glued back together. So, I run—I close myself off from feeling, from listening. I cannot feel their anguish or listen to their heartbreak. My own anguish—my own heartbreak—is too great to be added to theirs.

I have learned that I can hold on to him in my own way—letting go is not imperative and holding on is not unhealthy. I don't have to cut him from my life—I just have to realize that he is with me in a different way but with me nonetheless.

I have learned that not everyone can handle my pain—there are those who would rather avoid me than deal with me; perhaps it isn't that they are mean or uncaring but only scared and unsure. But I have also found a few who are willing to listen and are not repelled by my painful meanderings through the uncharted seas of grief. These few are like precious gems to be treasured forever.

I have learned that I am not alone—I am not the only parent to have lost a child. At the beginning, I felt that no one could possibly know what I was feeling—no one could have possibly endured this kind of total devastation. I realize now that there are others—many others—who have faced the indescribable. And though they did not lose my child, their child was equally precious to them. I feel a bond of shared sorrow with them—a bond ground in pain but strengthened by compassion and understanding…

I have learned that in trying to find someone responsible for our tragedy, I have felt justified in blaming God. But I've come to realize that He didn't give my son cancer and He didn't take my son's life—disease did. Now I can see that God was with us each step of the way and was there to take Jimmy from my arms into his own. And even though we didn't experience miraculous healing, perhaps our miracle took a more subtle form. From somewhere I got the strength to say no to more medical machinery and technology, from somewhere I got the strength to hold him during his last moments, from somewhere I got the strength to walk out of the hospital without him, and from somewhere I found the strength to struggle through the last thousand days. From somewhere—from somewhere.

I have learned that I can get lost in the mazes of "what if's" and "if only's" where there are only dead ends and more pain. The "could have beens" and "should have beens" are like a quicksand that is powerful and unmerciful in its futility. Somehow, I know I must free myself from its grip—I must find within myself the strength to stop wondering—to stop asking "Why, why, why?" For there are no answers. Maybe this is one of the most difficult of all lessons to master—the cold, hard fact that my son is gone and I will never know the reason—the why—of his death. It is a constant struggle I live with daily—the struggle to live with the hard realities and not with the lost possibilities…

I have learned that I am not going crazy even during the times I feel there is no other explanation. So many of the feelings I've experienced have been felt by almost every parent who has lost a child. This I have learned from reading and from listening. Though each person's grief is individual and unique, many of the characteristics of that grief are common to us all. No one is left unscathed—all of us bear the scars—but we are not crazy.

I have learned not to listen to others' prescriptions for my grief—their ideas of what I should feel or shouldn't feel are completely foreign to what I know is right for me. How can someone who has never walked in my shoes tell me what steps I need to take? There are certain situations that I cannot handle, and I should not be made to feel

Lessons from a Bereaved Mom

guilty for my inadequacy—I am inadequate and it's a fact I'm not ashamed of...

And I have learned that God does not forget that which is heavy upon our hearts. In His wisdom, He reaches out to caress and soothe. Through the people who have shared with us our loss, God has given us His love. I have learned that their deepest caring pours forth when I allow them in—when I let them see my ragged edges and my bleeding heart. But the truth makes you vulnerable and, for some reason, we hide behind that false face of well-being and wholeness. But eventually that face begins to crack and crumble, and it's then that we learn we are not alone—it's then that we truly begin to heal.

Someone hugs me and I feel God's compassion—someone listens and I feel God's understanding—someone cries with me and I feel God's sorrow—someone squeezes my hand and I feel God's strength—someone tells me something about my son and I feel God's hand lift the burden from my heart—someone lets me hold their newborn baby and I feel God's power—someone puts their little hand in mine and I feel God's presence— someone smiles a special smile and I feel God's joy—someone shares with me that which is most precious and I feel God's love. And someone says, "I love you" and I feel God's hope.

For where there is love, there is hope. And when I have once again found hope, then the victory will be ours—mine and my son's. For the renewal of hope is the salvation from despair.

And this, I have learned, is perhaps the most important lesson of all.

Twenty-Six Years Later

In communicating with Susan and asking her permission to include her words in this book, I asked her to write about Jimmy. This is what she wrote:

Jimmy was a kid who loved life. He was ornery and mischievous, and he drove his little sister crazy. He loved practical jokes. He once said that he wanted to be a scientist when he grew up. He would have made a good one.

He loved the Fourth of July because of the fireworks. We went to Arkansas every summer to see family, and he and my brother-in-law would build a "bomb" out of bottle rockets. They would work on it forever and were so excited when they finally lit it up. I can still hear the laughter.

We were going through our storeroom a few weeks ago, and I found some of his old school papers. He was trying to make the "J" in Jim like his dad does. It looks like the "J" that John Hancock used when he signed the Declaration of Independence.

Jimmy was a normal kid who loved his family, his friends, especially his best friend, Kris, and his dog. We put baby socks on Pup's feet when we brought Jim home from the hospital so Pup wouldn't scratch him welcoming him home. Somehow, dogs just know.

Jim was always doing karate moves after watching the movie The Karate Kid. Kylee, his sister, was usually the victim. He liked to jump up and touch the doorframes like Wilt Chamberlin or some other famous basketball player. It was just a few years ago that I finally painted over those beloved smudges. He made a zip line out of yarn and nailed it to the top of his bedroom wall so his GI Joe guys could slide down the stairs on it.

Not a day goes by that I don't think about him and wonder. He would have been forty years old this year. We will never know what he would have become, who he would have married, how many children he would have had, but I do know that he would have been a fine man who would have made a difference in this world of ours. I would give anything if he had just gotten the chance.

I also want to include some thoughts from Jimmy's dad, James. As he writes, fathers are sometimes overlooked, and this is a mistake for many reasons. Here is what Jimmy's dad wrote:

Lessons from a Bereaved Mom

I sometimes feel we dads get left out of people's understanding of the suffering over the loss of a child. When Jim passed away, someone had to be strong, and Susan couldn't do it. I had to make the phone calls and set up the arrangements. Later, I heard comments that made me feel people didn't believe I hurt as much as Susan. I hurt tremendously over the loss of Jim, but I kept the hurt inside. A father's grief might not be as visible and verbal, but I think in most situations, it's as deep as a mother's.

We were once told that the second year after the death of a child is the hardest. There may be some truth in that, but it has been twenty-six and a half years since Jim died, and I still hurt and miss him every day. I talk about him every chance I get. I also wonder what he would have become, who he would have married, and what children he would have had.

A neighbor once told me that Susan and I needed to adopt a boy. I asked him why and he said to take Jim's place.

In as nice a way as I could, I told him what a fool he was. If we had another boy of our own, or adopted one, he could not in any way take Jim's place.

We do now have one grandson, and both Susan and I do everything we can for him and enjoy spoiling him.

I will say this, when God gave our daughter and her husband their son, it was the closest to giving me Jim back as he could.

Certainly, Susan's and James words tell you a lot more about grief than I could. I would just like to remind readers of a few things:

- Don't feel you have to say anything profound to grieving parents. Attempting to do so can be more hurtful than helpful. For example, they might say their child is better off in heaven, but if you say it, it trivializes their loss. They want their child with them here on earth, not in heaven!

- Worse than saying the wrong thing is avoiding grieving parents altogether because you are afraid you will say the wrong thing.
- Avoid asking, "How are you?" That's an unfair question unless you know them well and are in a place to sit down and listen to how they are coping at this time. A big hug expresses more than words and does not require a fake "I'm fine" answer.
- Don't think that a person who has lost their child will be doing much better after a few months or even after a year. Grief is a roller coaster; it does not exhibit tidy stages that resolve. Many, many things will set grief off for years to come. Those who are grieving can patch over the holes in their hearts, but those patches spring leaks throughout a lifetime.
- Most people eventually learn to live with chronic grief and eventually experience happiness again, even if it tends to be fleeting.

Don't think I am the "expert" on grief. Everyone differs in how they grieve, and what helps them with their healing process also differs. When our grandson died, I certainly did not handle it flawlessly with our daughter. She was more private about her grief while I wanted to talk and share more openly. This urge was more for my own sake than for hers because this was not what she needed.

How will I handle it if our son, Tad, dies? It's impossible to predict. What I know intellectually and what I feel emotionally are two different things. Also, I know that the accumulation of losses and age can wear down your spirit. The only advantage I have is that I know bad things can happen to good people and that no one is absolved from sorrow and loss, so I will not suffer from the "Why me? Why my child?" questions that haunts so many grieving parents. For now, I work hard to treasure each conversation with

Tad, enjoy the beauty of nature around me, and try not to reflect too far ahead. Each hour and day with our loved ones is precious, and I do not want to waste time on anticipatory grief.

Personal Reflections

One sunny Saturday in late May toward the end of my ten years as a pediatric oncology social worker, I was sitting by the side of our pool writing a pile of graduation cards and a pile of bereavement cards for "my" families from the hospital when it suddenly struck me what a strangely normal dichotomy this was.

The teens I worked with and loved saw life at its best and worst. They died many times over the death of a dream, the death of a career, the death of a body image due to the loss of a leg or hair. I went to more funerals than I care to remember during my ten years at SLCH and later returned to the Midwest for a few more.

Some funerals were very personal, some were formal where everyone tried to keep a stiff upper lip, and some allowed weeping and wailing. I thought this was the most natural way to react to the death of a child. I was always very touched when a group of our teens was brave enough to attend the funeral of one of "their" own.

I observed at one of the teen's funerals that whether they were black or white, younger or older, male or female, rich or poor, these teens were bonded together through their grief and love for one another.

Professionals often comment that "The family is in denial" about parents or their teenagers who have life-threatening conditions, but who is really in denial? During a training session for new counselors at a camp for children and teens with cancer, an American Cancer Society staff member kept emphasizing that these were normal kids and that we were going to treat them that way.

One counselor in my car, Mark Varady, a teen being treated for cancer himself, said, "Who is she trying to kid? We aren't normal. Nothing about our lives is normal, but we have to pretend it is around our peers in order to be accepted. It would be nice to go somewhere where we didn't have to pretend for once."

I realized that the allegations of "denial" were often due to a lack of understanding. It wasn't unusual for a teen to want to talk about their death one day and about high school graduation the next. I found this perfectly normal. An excerpt from the book *This Narrow Space* written by pediatric oncologist Elisha Waldman beautifully defines what I have known for a long time: "I have often found that up to the very end, patients and their families are able to simultaneously understand that death is inevitable and to continue to hope for a cure. F. Scott Fitzgerald famously wrote that 'The test of a first-rate intelligence is the ability to hold two opposing ideas in mind at the same time and still retain the ability to function.' I'm learning that this is part of what it means to be human, and what keeps my patients and their families going from day to day."

Watching the movie *Allure*, it occurred to me that the life it depicts—so hollow, where life revolves around nothing but how you look, including plastic surgery, facelifts, and liposuction—is the dark side of life. By contrast, being with these special teens isn't dark at all.

Personal Reflections

There is so much depth to the lives of teens with cancer that most people are afraid to step into the reservoir of pain, joy, love, compassion, understanding, and friendship they feel and experience. What a privilege to have the opportunity to be such an intimate part of their lives, and the lives of their families, at such a crucial time.

Giving Difficult News to a Family

I was often asked by our oncologists to be in the room when they told a family their child had cancer or had relapsed. In fact, the head of the oncology department, Dr. Theresa Vietti, used to frantically page me when she was going to talk to a family. Although she was brilliant medically, Dr. Vietti knew she lacked the skill to give the news gently. She wanted to make sure I was there to pick up the pieces.

An important lesson I learned was that you can give good news anywhere, but when you are giving parents information that will be difficult to hear, what you tell them, where you tell them, and how you tell them will remain with them for the rest of their lives.

I know physicians are often in a rush, but whenever possible, I tried to see that the discussion took place in a private setting, that the parents were not greatly outnumbered by staff, and that the family was allowed to feel both grief and hope. It was important to give them permission to be upset, to say things like, "I appreciate how frightening it is to hear this news."

It was also important not to give them too much information right away because they simply could not hear it. Their minds were frozen on "Your child has cancer" or "Your child has relapsed."

They needed time to grieve, but it was also important that I return in an hour or two to answer their questions. Holding onto the questions that arose for even a day was unbearable.

Having taken notes during the initial meeting, I would tell the family what I had learned, but I discovered that once you've worked in the oncology environment for a length of time, you get used to using terminology that non-medical people might not understand but are too embarrassed to admit.

In some ways, I was better at figuring out what parents didn't understand earlier in my career than later, when I had become used to the language. I'll never forget one family we kept saying things to like, "When her counts are up…" and "When her counts are down…" Finally, after about four or five days, the mother said to me, "What are counts?" She did not know we were talking about blood counts. We had wasted days trying to educate her when vital information was going over her head.

A common staff error was to be unrealistically cheerful at this emotionally fraught time. The goal was to try to uplift the family, but it was better to be kindly honest and compassionate. The family deserved the truth even when some of the reality could wait until they had adjusted and had been connected with appropriate support. How to give parents realistic, honest answers without destroying all hope is a constant challenge for physicians and staff.

We were constantly weighing what to put in our information booklets. We searched for a balance between what would give hope to the parents of the newly diagnosed child yet be honest and a source of education and support. If the potential reality of the future wasn't tempered by hope and encouragement, they might run from the truth and the support they needed.

I found at that time and have observed many times since that the educational and emotional level of the family needs to be taken into consideration when planning your discussion. I remember the day, years later, that I was diagnosed with breast cancer. The nurse gave me a booklet with a tab in it and said, "I don't want you to read beyond that tab." That gave me a laugh. I'd been in the medical field for years—of course I was going to read beyond that tab. That's why it's good to have different reading materials for different phases. We can't stop the parents of a newly diagnosed child from getting on the internet, but we can do our best not to throw those materials in their faces.

Physicians and staff are the family's lifeline of hope and truth. If the medical people handle the situation appropriately, gratitude for their compassionate expertise will remain with the family about to walk into that private consultation room for the rest of their lives. The opposite, of course, is also true. Giving difficult news is an awesome responsibility but also a wonderful opportunity to make a significant difference at a crucial crossroads in a family's life.

My Farewell

Some things in life are hard to do. Others are gut wrenching. That's the only way I know to describe how hard it was to break the news that I was leaving SLCH. I left not because I was "burned out" but because I was taking a job in the pediatric bone marrow transplant unit at All Children's Hospital in St. Petersburg, Florida. Our five children were all grown and out of the house, so it was time to take the leap and make the move to Florida to be close to our son Tad, his wife, Gina, and our new grandbaby, Tyler. We had known for a long time that we wanted to move to Florida someday, but we also knew from my work in the field of hospice before SLCH and pediatric oncology that sometimes "someday" never comes.

I have been asked if I left SLCH because pediatric oncology was so depressing. My response has always been, "No, it was never depressing. Depressing is working in a job you don't like with people you don't like. Working with children who have cancer was sad at times, but it was never depressing."

I loved the people I worked with, and I loved their families. I was fortunate. I always knew that what I was doing was meaningful. But there is often more than one season of life, and what I didn't know at the time was that I had another important season and reason ahead of me, working with children and adults with Prader-Willi syndrome, the disability our son, Matt, was born with. Matt is alive and doing well at age forty-five, but when he was diagnosed, the life expectancy for someone with Prader-Willi syndrome was only a few decades.

On a volunteer basis, Al and I had started the Missouri state chapter for PWS. I served on the national board and eventually became president. By then, I was known for my writings on the syndrome. A couple of years after our move to Florida, I was offered a job as the executive director of the national organization, the Prader-Willi Syndrome Association (USA), which I held for the next ten years; I then served as director of medical and coordinator of research for PWSA (USA) for another ten years until I retired.

The syndrome is too complex to go into here, but Prader-Willi syndrome is the most common known genetic cause of life-threatening obesity in children. Children with PWS have a dysfunction of the hypothalamus that causes multiple problems including a constant sense of hunger. PWS is genetic but is not inherited except in rare cases.

My future fate as executive director of PWSA (USA) was not clear to me at the time we moved and did not diminish the anguish of our leaving. When Al called to tell Corey Peterson's parents we were moving several years after Corey had died, he talked to Pam, who was dealing with cancer herself. He heard Pete in the background saying over and over, "I don't want to hear it! I don't want to hear it!"

When we told Todd Wright, the young man we had followed through treatment since he was a teenager and who was back in the hospital now at age twenty-five, he began sobbing. When we had to leave the room, he was still crying.

I cried more that last month than at almost any other time in my life. Every day I was moved to tears by a card a child brought or a special note a family wrote, and every day I had to say goodbye to someone special not knowing if I would ever see them again.

My last day at SLCH was like most days in that it was frantically busy. At my last official (thank God) farewell, I received a gold watch for my ten years of employment. This farewell wasn't nearly as hard as the others because it was with the other social workers

Personal Reflections

and non-oncology professionals. Although I liked and would miss nearly everyone, I did not have the tremendous bond of pain and passion with these people that I'd developed with the oncology staff and families.

After packing up my office, it was 8:00 p.m. I had promised to stop at the summer camp for children and teens who had cancer to say my farewells, so even though we were exhausted, Al and I drove out.

The kids were already in their cabins, so we walked to each one. When I went to the little girls' cabin, three of the girls sang and danced for me. One kept asking, "Why are you leaving? Why are you moving?" Little Erin started sobbing, so I carried her down with me to the teen area where the teens sang me a song.

There my heart broke anew. Ray, a poor fifteen-year-old with little in the way of family life, turned away with tears running down his cheeks. Brandon, whom I had followed since he was seven years old and who was now fourteen, could not stop sobbing. Chrissy had just relapsed and was facing a long road ahead. Her arms crossed, the look on her face said, "I'm tough, and I'm going to protect myself," but it was contradicted by the tears trickling down her cheeks. Bill and Eddie, both of whom had become leaders in the group, had their arms around several crying teens.

Adam's mother, who was there as a volunteer camp counselor, said to me, "Jan, look around the room at the legacy you're leaving behind."

John Randles, always one to attempt to lighten the moment when it gets too heavy, looked at all the crying kids and said, "Yeah, Jan, look at the path of destruction you're leaving behind!"

My eyes blurred with tears, I took one last look at "my kids" and wondered which of them I might see again. Walking out that door was one of the hardest things I have ever done.

The next day, Eddie Greenhill, who was twenty-one at the time and in college, stopped by my office to pick up the desk we had promised to give him and to say his goodbyes. We stopped long enough to do a "I remember when…" Eddie had been with us through four relapses at that point and many, many sad and happy times.

The last two things I carefully wrapped and lovingly placed in the car were a clock that the CURE bereavement group had given me in a wooden case inscribed with, "Thanks from all your angels—8/14/94" that still sits on my desk today, twenty-four years later, and a Precious Moments statue Corey's parents had given me of a hitchhiking boy and an angel driving a car with a license plate that said "Going my way."

As we drove away from St. Louis Children's Hospital for the last time, I said to the clouds, "Yes, my angels, today I'm going to Florida, but some day, we are all 'going your way.'"

Cancer Hits Home

Although both my husband, Al, and I have been treated for cancer since I worked at St. Louis Children's Hospital, I cannot compare what we've gone through to the agonizing experience of having a child with cancer.

Our "child," Tad, was fifty-two years old and 6'4" tall when he was diagnosed in early 2018 with an advanced cancer of the head and neck. Tad and his wife, Gina, are COO and CEO of a rehabilitation hospital in Dallas, Texas, called **icare♥**. Although Tad is a competent adult, your child is your child. No matter how old he might be, you want to do all you can to protect him from physical and emotional pain, but that is virtually impossible when you're dealing with cancer. The older your child is, the less chance you have of cradling him in your arms and telling him everything will be okay. If the doctor doesn't tell him the reality, the internet will, and there's no chance to buffer what might lie ahead.

In addition, as the parent of a grown child, you walk a fine line between doing and saying what is helpful and overstepping your boundaries. Fortunately, Tad is exceptionally kind, while sweet Gina understood my need to attempt to be helpful.

With Tad, as is true in many cases, there appeared to be no rhyme or reason to his diagnosis. Typically, people with his type of cancer are avid smokers and drinkers, but Tad has never smoked, and it is extremely rare for him to take a drink. Tad looks very strong because he works out regularly at the gym and eats well, but he was already dealing with an adult form of muscular dystrophy plus several autoimmune disorders.

Tad has lived his entire life helping others through various forms of personal, business, and faith-based outreaches, giving hope to the seeming hopeless and motivating people to be and do more with their lives. His diagnosis was traumatic not only to his immediate family members and close friends but also to his more than five thousand followers on Facebook.

I hadn't really cried since our grandson, Adam, was killed in an accident, not even when I was diagnosed with breast cancer, but I cried over Tad's diagnosis. I couldn't even ask myself, "How could such a good, kind person get this horrible disease?" because I had known too many beautiful children and teens who had suffered this way. No one was—no one is—immune.

The night he was diagnosed, Tad and Gina asked their young adult children, Tyler, twenty-five, and Taina, twenty-three, to come home. They wanted to break the news to them in person. They all lay in their king-size bed huddled together, talking, crying, and watching the opening of the Olympics, which Gina loves.

Later, Tad told me the love of his life, Gina, wondered if they should sell the hospital and go live in their vacation house in the Bahamas. Tad told her that he'd lived his entire life caring about other people and didn't regret it. He said he didn't need to go into seclusion on an island now and would rather stay around the people he loves.

I talked to our sweet grandson Tyler, who told me he was calling all the young adults Tad had mentored (several lived with them at times) when they were teenagers. Tyler was trying to be strong for his friends, but he needed support himself. Summer, Tyler's fiancé, tried to cheer him up, but when he woke up the morning after learning about his dad's diagnosis and she looked at him with a big smile on her face, he wanted to say, "Stop smiling!"

I told our daughter Tracy, "I remember sitting on the swing with Tad outside your house the day Adam died. Tad was crying and said he would do anything to take your sadness away. I'm sure you feel the same way about him now." Through her tears, Tracy responded, "I absolutely do!"

The night after Tad was diagnosed, we took our youngest grandchildren, Noelle and Rocco, our daughter Sarah's children, on a planned trip to the circus. Driving home, eight-year-old Rocco said that the strongmen balancing act reminded him of Uncle Tad. Then he started sobbing and said, "I just want Tad to stay safe."

I told our oldest grandson, Mike, our daughter Tina's son, what his little cousin Rocco had said, and he responded, "Aww. Poor Rocco. Tell him that Tad is the strongest person we know. If he can tear phonebooks in half and break bricks [something Tad did in his youth ministry outreach days with a group called Strike Force], he can get through this—although Rocco probably doesn't know what a phonebook is."

Tad told his sister Sarah that he has no regrets, that he's lived so intensely that he's lived the lives of four people. He said the hardest part is how sad this is making the people he loves. Gina told him she didn't want to live without him, and he told her she has to be strong for their children—and the grandchildren who might come after him.

During the first few weeks after diagnosis, due to the agonizing daily changes in Tad's situation and each new specialist giving even more dire information on his prognosis, I felt my heart breaking a little more each day.

Although I desperately wanted to, I did not rush to Tad's side. I knew Tad, Gina, Tyler, and Taina needed private time together. They certainly didn't need a pathetic mother/ grandmother staying in their home, looking for ways to help, and possibly being too intrusive.

Finally, when Tad could no longer eat and had to have a PEG tube inserted into his stomach to provide essential nutrition, Al and I headed for Dallas, and I stayed for three weeks to help with the complicated medication and tube feedings.

Tad kept working out at the gym at 5:30 every morning and going to the rehab hospital to work despite how bad he felt. This included terrible pain from the radiation on his tongue and down his throat, constant secretions he couldn't swallow and had to spit or suction out, and the usual nausea and tiredness associated with chemotherapy.

We would do the early morning medications and liquid tube feedings, then I would go to the hospital with him to volunteer and help with the same noontime medication and feeding ritual. Late afternoon, we would rush to the various hospitals where he got daily radiation and weekly chemotherapy. Once home, we would begin the medication and tube feeding ritual again, after which he would collapse and fall into an exhausted sleep. While attempting to sleep, he frequently had to wake up to suction the horrible choking secretions out of his throat so he could breathe.

It was painful to see how non-complaining and kind Tad was throughout this ordeal. During my time in Texas and afterwards, he pushed himself beyond normal human limits. Part of me wanted him to snap at me or get angry at someone. Why? The more he reminded me of my oncology children and teens like Kalilah, Darren, Corey, and Eddie, the more I feared for his life. For a long time, I have had the superstition that those children and teens who are too good to be true are not meant to be in this world for long—they are sent here to teach us about goodness and courage. Thus, I wanted Tad to be a little bit bad. I really didn't—I really don't—want him to be one of those special angels.

Shortly after Tad completed treatment, he confided in me that he was having concerning symptoms. I was painfully aware that like the children and their families in oncology, we were going to fear the elusive killer called cancer was hiding around the corner just waiting to terrorize us again for a very long time.

Were flu symptoms really just the flu? Were extreme tiredness and night sweats the residual effects of radiation or the beginning signs of a relapse? Was the new pain just a pulled muscle or was it metastatic bone cancer?

Because the original symptoms were not identified as cancer until it had spread, it was impossible to trust our own judgment or even the judgment of some of the experts in the field that the new symptoms were nothing to be worried about.

Everyone tried to make us feel better by coming up with plausible (and sometimes not plausible) reasons for the symptoms in their attempts to ease our concerns. They said, "It's probably just…" and we agreed, "Yes, it's probably just…" but we didn't really believe it. During the day, we could minimize our fears by staying busy, but in the quiet of the night, the terrifying shadow of that elusive killer crept into our consciousness and our dreams.

In October of 2018, just three months after completing treatment, a PET scan and biopsies confirmed that Tad's cancer had spread to both lungs. Tad told me that after he got the news, he and Gina took Taina (she was working at the hospital) into the back to tell her. After they all had a good cry, Tad walked out and encountered an outpatient named Mandy.

A quadruple amputee, Mandy had lost all four limbs a year earlier due to an infection. She attributes Tad's and Gina's rehab hospital to saving her life by doing a miraculous job of rehabbing her. She and her husband were very sad to hear Tad's news, but Tad told her, "How can I be discouraged after seeing you?"

I believe in synchronicity, that the right people come into your life at the right time, and I believe Mandy was meant to walk into the hospital at that very moment.

As I mentioned before, I worked with cancer too long to be shocked by Tad's metastasis to the lungs. I've also worked with too many amazing, loving children and teens who died to think my own child can't die. It just leaves me with deep sadness, and Al feels the same way. We can busy ourselves and not think about it for a while, but our thoughts always come back to Tad.

On Halloween, it was great to see pictures of Tad and Gina in costume and having fun, but I know that every special event from now on will cause us to wonder, "Is this his last…?" Of course, he could be the one to beat the odds, and it helps most of the family cope to believe this will be true, but my way of coping is to prepare for the worst and rejoice if he does indeed beat the odds.

Tad created a gut-wrenchingly honest Facebook page (Tad Tomaseski) detailing his journey through treatment and wrote a number of blog posts available at #GetUp, #StrongLove, #ATadBitStrong, #RoundTwo, and #PureLove that reflect his philosophies on life. Tad's goal was, and is, to try to help others as he goes through this ordeal. The following excerpts give a glimpse into the physical and emotional trials of treatment and the heart and soul of our son Tad.

Tad's Facebook Post 2/19/18

My cancer is not an easy one. It scares me. It has spread to some bad areas. My treatment side effects are going to be awful and there are no guarantees, but there are people with much worse cancers than me going through much worse treatments with much worse prognoses…One person in particular I get to hug at work every day.

My muscular dystrophy, diagnosed years before I was diagnosed with cancer, scares me. The dysferlin in my muscles continues to fail, leaving the muscles in my legs, arms, and lats eroding away like some creature comes at night chewing away at them from one end to the other. But as a child I played games with a young man with a much worse form of muscular dystrophy that not only disabled him but eventually took his ability to breathe and took his life…His two brothers had the same MD, and they both passed away as well.

So when I'm feeling sorry for myself, I go DOWN for the COUNT…I count my blessings, and that gives me strength to GET UP!

Tad's Facebook post 3/19/18

What did I do when the alarm went off at 4:30 a.m. and I felt horrible, nauseous, throat like a flame thrower was on it all night, tongue like I bit it as hard as ever, still have IV in my hand, taste buds are gone to the point that everything tastes horrible, even water tastes awful, so it's another day of force feeding and force drinking to stay alive, knowing I have another bout of chemo and radiation today, really don't want to face another day of this, and they say the worst is yet to come, I'm just in round one…I lie there just long enough to count my blessings and then I GET UP…Head to the gym…Play my custom GET UP track by James R. Smith III over and over and over again and push myself through the workout and make something of this day…Because being knocked down is a reality, lying there feeling beaten half to death is real, not wanting to face the life that just knocked me down again is just being honest with myself. I hear people say "Kick cancer's ass." That's a nice thought, but the reality is that cancer is kicking my ass. It's knocking me down minute by minute, and much of the time I feel like a bloody beaten mess, but CANCER IS NOT WINNING…Because staying down is not an option for me…I've fought too hard for this life to give up…GET UP! GET UP! GET UP!

Tad's Facebook post 3/31/18

My secret weapon against cancer is my mom, Janalee. ☺ She too is a cancer survivor. Ironically enough, she was in the midst of writing her book about cancer when I was diagnosed. She was the hematology/oncology social worker for St. Louis Children's Hospital and is writing about the amazing spirits the children had through it all and the incredible things they said. She was also the abuse case worker for the Department of Children and Family services in Illinois and the executive director for the Prader-Willi Syndrome Association. She has led countless volunteer movements like the bereavement group for parents of murdered children, etc. She came to stay with us for three weeks to help while I'm going through treatment. She's been helping with all my tube feedings and keeping track of the many meds I am on and helping chauffeur me around for my treatments. She couldn't stand to be away from her baby boy while I'm going through all this. She is my rock in life. From the time I could first talk, she is the person who planted in me so much love for others, compassion for others, and appreciation for life by teaching me that no matter how bad it is, somebody has it even worse.

Janalee and Tad

She gave me the tools needed in the toolbox of my soul to be able to GET UP when bad times hit hard. She taught me to never leave people you love angry and to always resolve things before parting because something could happen and you'd never see them again to reconcile. I could go on and on, but she is just the most impactful woman I have ever known and she just so happens to be my mom. ☺ Many people have had their lives dramatically impacted by her work and her servant's heart; she is loved and treasured around the world. She taught me early on that the greatest thing you can do with your life is to serve others less fortunate... And if you're not doing this, then why are you even here? If you ever feel like you've done enough for others, just compare notes with her. It's enough to make anybody want to up their game.

Tad's Facebook Post 4/08/18

Sunday is no exception. Was down after another tough night and morning but made myself GET UP and get a workout in and then head home for a series of dry heaving holding a bowl. Got more nausea meds in me now; hopefully they'll kick in shortly.

I can only imagine what sort of story people are writing in their minds about this guy at the gym who "hocks a loogie" into paper towels after every set. (My salivary glands are dead so these horrible secretions that are like half dried glue mixed with spider webs continue to build in my throat and are accelerated when I work out or talk. If I don't get them out, I will basically suffocate.) On top of that, this guy has some strange protuberance sticking way out from one spot on his stomach (this is my feeding tube, which isn't concealed at all), and he can be found at times in the locker room dry heaving over the sinks.

I can only wonder what story they must make up in their heads, but what they think doesn't stop me. How I feel doesn't stop me. It knocks me down OFTEN, but I don't stay down. I always have to find a way to GET UP.

Whatever has you down today, don't let it keep you down. It's time to GET UP and do something...anything...that is positive movement. We have to keep moving forward.

Tad's Facebook Post 4/23/18

I thought I'd hit bottom last post, but apparently it was just a ledge I landed on before falling in the pit. I now weight 179 pounds (I lost 37 pounds, 25 to 30 of it muscle). Came into the oncologist to decide whether to re-hospitalize again because it was absolute agonizing hell at home. We're running a couple of bags of fluid and made some more changes to the plan and I'm going to try to stay home another night. At this point it's sheer 24/7 survival mode, hanging on the ropes, gasping for air. Gonna make it, gonna continue to GET UP, but the fight is fierce, and my opponent is pulling no punches whatsoever. Whatever health is in your body today, give thanks and rejoice in it, no matter what isn't going the way you want it to, because I can tell you that when your health is gone, none of the rest of that stuff matters one bit!

Heartbreaking Text 4/25/18

It was sketchy but made it through a short day at work [yesterday]. Went in today again. Terrible night last night but a tiny bit better day today. A very small spark of light. Hoping for a tolerable night. It's been so long.

Got down a tiny bit of food today and went back to tube feed for the day. Hoping to get off TPN in next couple of days. Been doing a massive drop of meds. Zero pain meds. Gotta make positive progress. Can't go on like it has been recently. Not tolerable in any way. Eating away at my soul.

Tad's Facebook Post 5/13/18

For three months, every day was worse than the one before. Even when it didn't seem possible it could get worse, it did, over and over again. But I'm glad to announce that for the last seven days, each day has been a little better than the day before. I have a long, long, long way to go, but I am so thankful for movement in a positive direction.

At my lowest I was down nearly 40 pounds at 178, and those who know me understand I didn't carry extra weight I could afford to lose. I am still down 20 pounds of muscle and am very weak but getting a little stronger each day. I have not used my feeding tube for three weeks and Monday morning they are removing it, which is a huge milestone for me. I'm on a very limited diet due to residual tongue and throat pain I am fighting, having zero saliva as glands were killed and not back yet, and having almost no taste buds. All were killed and have to grow back. I am also off all prescription meds.

Those who know me well know that I have always been more emotional than the average man. When you have been as sick as I have been as long as I have been, with things always getting worse, seemingly little things become very emotional milestones. Since I was diagnosed, I have been in doctor's offices or hospitals getting treatments or procedures every day. Once I finished treatment, I had to go to my chemo doctor every week and get blood draws to check my levels. For four weeks after treatment, everything continued to get worse to the point that I can't begin to describe the condition I was in. But on Monday, my doctor told me something that made me so emotional, it's still hard to say without tearing up. He told me I didn't have to come back for two weeks and my levels were so good I wouldn't need a blood draw next time.

I'm sure that doesn't sound like much to most people, but to hear I was healthy enough to not see a doctor for two weeks was the best news I've had since before I was diagnosed in February… Anyway, this post is already too long, but I wanted to give a solid update and thank the thousands of you around the globe who have been encouraging me, praying for me, believing for me, and loving me through this. I read every single comment and message every one of you takes the time to post. They are all food to my soul. Thank you. I love and appreciate you all.

"FAILURE IS ONLY POSSIBLE IF YOU QUIT...DON'T EVER GIVE UP...GET UP!!!"

Tad's tattoo

Tad's Blog Post, "A Broken Tongue Speaks Out"

Throughout my life, I have been a "silent sufferer." I've seldom talked about my struggles, fears, pain, or times of hopelessness. I would rather people only see my seemingly optimistic spirit because I have not wanted them to see the incredible struggle behind the silence.

I find it ironic that this cancer has stemmed from a tumor at the base of my tongue because I feel I have always held my tongue. I have stayed silent about my struggles, but now I know in the depths of my soul that holding my tongue will help no one, including myself.

I am hoping that the words in this blog that come forth from a broken, diseased tongue can bring hope and healing to someone's soul, maybe even to my own. Sometimes just knowing that we are not the only ones beaten down on the mat, that we aren't lying down there alone, can be enough to keep us hoping we can continue to GET UP.

If we are too proud, private, or shy to share our struggles and down times, leaving others to think we always feel up, then we also leave them to think they are alone and that there might be no hope for them to ever GET UP. There is currently a tremendous increase of depression in society due to the presence of social media making other people's lives seem so perfect that it convinces people that nobody else has problems…This just isn't true.

I told Gina that I don't have a choice…I have to go through this cancer. But I do have a choice of HOW I will go through it and what the outcome of my HOW will be. I don't agree with the thought that God allows everything to happen for a reason. I don't believe God gave me or anybody else cancer or the other terrible things that happen to us in order to accomplish some divine purpose. But I do believe my faith enables me to find purpose while going through it. My purpose is to use this struggle to help others GET UP, and in turn that will also give me even more reason to GET UP.

…Let me be clear that despite this and other tragedies in my life, I count myself a man blessed beyond belief. I have such tremendous love for and from so many wonderful people. Know that if you are one of them, you make my life blessed, and you are one of the reasons I GET UP!

Tad's Blog Post, "Real Courage"

I think it's okay to be afraid. I want you to know that I am scared. I live with fear. Courage is not the absence of fear or the denial of reality.

Real courage is when you are horribly scared, wanting to lie there and not move, frozen in fear as though a giant grizzly bear is circling you for the kill…but at some point, you decide to GET UP anyway and keep moving forward, even though you are scared every step of the way. That takes courage.

There is a time for fear and worry. But you can't keep lying there until that fear and worry go away because they might never go away and that's okay…So, sooner or later, GET UP anyway and go forward. The more you GET UP and go forward in spite of your fear and worry, the less your fear will control you, and the worry will move from the front of your mind to the back of your mind.

I also think it's okay to feel sorry for yourself…for a period of time. But sooner or later, you have to GET UP anyway or feeling sorry for yourself will keep you DOWN for the COUNT.

This part has been rooted deep in my soul from early childhood. I was fortunate to grow up in a home where I was continually put in the presence of people less fortunate than me in so many ways. Granted, we were by no means wealthy by worldly standards. My parents worked hard to put clothes on our back and a roof over our heads, but I never felt we lacked anything because I saw how many others had so much less.

I remember being in Joliet, Illinois, at the home of my foster brother's biological family one Christmas Eve. They were a family of six kids with a single mom working long hours for very little money, sleeping three to a bedroom with mom on the couch in a tiny home. I remember each of them receiving their Christmas stocking, an athletic tube sock filled with oranges, nuts in the shell, and a couple of small toys that you would pick up in a dollar store…And they were so excited and thankful to get it.

How could I ever feel as though I lacked anything?

I experienced firsthand the prejudice, verbal abuse, and hatred they suffered simply because of the color of their skin. My foster brother's younger brother was my best friend. Our neighbors, the Weavers, were extreme racists. The young boy and girl would do and say such cruel things to us. When I was eleven, my mom told me we were moving and that we wouldn't have to put up with the Weavers anymore. I said, "But Mom, no matter where we live, there will always be another kind of Weaver."

How could I ever feel disadvantaged?

I spent hours playing games with disabled children while we drove them to their doctor's appointments. My mom would tell me, "They don't have friends because other kids are cruel and won't take the time to get to know them." It was up to me to be their friend.

How could I ever feel unloved?

I spent a lot of time with incredibly beautiful children who were going through terrible cancer treatments, and many did not survive. They didn't get to experience a love of their lives, have children, or become adults. Yet they were so full of love and had so much fight in their spirits.

How could I ever feel I have it that bad?

So, whenever I am DOWN for the COUNT...which earlier today I was...I count my blessings.

Tad's Blog Post, "Why Me?"

This is a very natural question when life delivers a tragic blow that knocks you down hard, particularly someone who has made great efforts to be "good." It seems especially unfair when it happens to someone who genuinely doesn't deserve it while "bad" people never seem to get "what they deserve."

Recently, people who know me have been struggling to accept what's happening to me. They've watched how I've taken care of my body and health in ways that most people don't. They've also witnessed the depth of my love and caring for others, and it has left them confused and wondering "Why Tad?"

Many people of faith are taught that good things will happen to those who believe and do right while bad things are reserved for those who don't believe and do wrong. So, when tragedy hits, these people are left wondering "What did I do wrong to deserve this?" This leaves them knocked down, crawling around the mat, trying to find what they did wrong, searching for their own guilt. These people think that if they can find out what they did wrong, they can make amends with God and He will take it all away.

Others turn their backs completely on their faith, wondering, "How could a loving God let this happen?"

This is natural. There is no shame in asking "Why me?" It does not show a lack of faith to question and be angry with God.

People of faith often struggle hard with "Why me?" as many are taught that only good things will happen to those who believe. Many are taught that the answer to tragedy is to deny what is happening to them because if they speak about it, then they lack faith and will not be delivered. They are told to confess the opposite of what is really happening as truth or they lack faith and it will be their own fault that they are not healed.

Let me assure you, this philosophy doesn't stem from faith but rather from man's desire to be in control, which quite honestly defies the very definition of faith. It says that we can control God and the world around us by our own actions.

This belief does not resonate with me. I don't believe I will be delivered from cancer or muscular dystrophy by denying that it is happening and declaring things are actually going the way I want them to. I don't see God as a puppet whose strings I can pull to get what I want. It would be nice if that were true, as I would be in control and I could make it all stop.

Don't get me wrong; the power of belief and a positive attitude are strong, so don't read this as opposing these things, but I believe that good things can happen to all people and bad things can happen to all people, regardless of how "good" or "bad" we are.

I grew up watching sweet, precious, innocent children who believed in God and had never done anything wrong die of cancer, and I have also watched uncaring people with no faith and questionable character be healed of cancer.

I have witnessed children born disabled in ways we cannot imagine who are the most beautiful, loving people I have ever met, and I have also met many people born perfectly normal who suffer no health problems whatsoever who are filled with hatred and completely self-absorbed.

I could go on with more examples, but they would all lead to the same conclusion…LIFE IS JUST NOT FAIR, and our actions do not always determine our outcomes. When we accept this, we can get past "Why me?" and get on with "What should I do now?"

We can choose to accept that life is not fair, what is still happening is not fair, we don't deserve it, and we can't do anything about it…And then we can decide what it is we can control and make it our reason to GET UP and move forward.

We cannot control or change the tragedy that has happened. Many times, as in my case, we can't even control what tragedy is continuing to happen. What we can control is how we go through it.

Tad's Blog Post, "Get Up Heroes"

We've all seen movies where the hero dives into the water to save somebody who's down and dying. The hero heroically pulls the victim up and breathes life into his or her lungs, saving the individual from certain death.

Everyone loves a hero—this is why news stations work so hard to find a hero to spotlight when tragedy strikes—but there's another group of heroes that saves many lives every day in a very different way. These individuals are heroes because they *save themselves* in the midst of tragedy. Then, through the story of their heroic rescue of themselves, they inspire others to save themselves.

If you were to look at the lives of any one of my three sisters today, all experiencing such joy and love, you could easily find yourself thinking, "Wow! I wish I had their lives!"

I promise, if you knew what they've gone through and in some ways still are going through, if you had to suffer what they've suffered to get to where they are, you wouldn't be willing to endure it. Their devastating knockdowns are their stories to tell, but I suspect that most women would have been so scarred and damaged that they would either have given up completely or gone on to live tragic lives.

All three of my sisters have been knocked down, over and over again, yet all three have managed to GET UP and GO ON with life and become amazing women full of love. Therefore, they are also surrounded by the love of many others. They are true heroes to me, and their heroism inspires me when I am down to GET UP and keep moving.

It's important to have heroes. It's nice to have heroes like famous people from history or people you've read about in books or religious figures like Jesus, but you also need heroes you can follow closely today, people who have suffered something as bad or even worse than you who managed to GET UP and GO ON and not let tragedy doom them to live tragic lives. These real-life heroes who are close enough to be "touchable" make it seem that much more possible that we too can GET UP just like them.

Then, one day soon, it will be your turn to "breathe life" into someone else by sharing your story of how you managed to GET UP when life knocked you down, and you will be their hero.

This has been a tough week for me. I got knocked down hard again. My mouth, tongue, and throat became so damaged from the radiation that everything I tried to swallow, even water, felt like swallowing broken glass. Then, on Monday, I stopped being able to swallow altogether and choked on everything. I spent four days in the hospital and had to have a feeding tube put in through the wall of my abdomen into my stomach. I have not eaten for eight days. I now pour my medicines and my liquid nutrition into this tube to get it into my stomach to prevent me from dying from lack of nutrition.

This has been a devastating blow. I wanted so badly for this not to happen, but by the end, it was so painful to swallow that I would just put on my headphones, play my GET UP montage over and over again, and force down food with tears running down my face from the excruciating pain. To know I was only a third of the way through my radiation treatments and that things would only get worse was a big hit that knocked me down hard this week.

But you know what? I didn't stay down. All my real-life heroes who have gone before me breathed life into me, filling my spirit with hope that I could GET UP and keep moving forward. First day out of the hospital, I was at the gym working out, big old feeding tube hanging out of my stomach and all, and then I went straight into work to continue to serve and love the patients in our hospital, helping them GET UP too.

You might feel knocked down right now. I want you to know that I am right there with you. I know exactly how you feel. I want you to know that my sisters and my other heroes managed to GET UP, and so can you and I.

If we are not enough to inspire you, then keep looking for someone who does. Don't give up. Just searching for heroes to inspire you is a good sign that you want to GET UP and that you're not giving up. Keep searching, don't give up, and I promise you, sooner or later, you will GET UP…And when you do, you too will be a hero!

Tad's Facebook Post "Pure Love" after He Relapsed 10/27/18

Life is not fair…That is true.

Life is beautiful…That is also true.

Don't ever let the unfair part of life keep you from embracing the most beautiful part of life.

What is the most beautiful part of life?
Without question, it is LOVE. I don't mean the kind of love commonly pictured, though that love is amazing.
I am speaking of the LOVE that passes all understanding.

The LOVE that is given with nothing expected in return…
And even when nothing is given in return,
it continues to be given over and over and over again.

It's the LOVE that does not discriminate whom it is given to…It is given without consideration.

It is the LOVE that cannot be earned or deserved…
It is given freely without qualification.

It is PURE LOVE, and it is the most beautiful part of life.

You can't search and find it...You won't find somebody who will give it to you to keep...Because if you think it is about receiving it, you missed the entire point and can't even understand what you were given and therefore can't experience the PURE part of LOVE. You will also continually search to find more of it because you think you have to receive it to experience it.

You will experience the MOST BEAUTIFUL part of life when you realize that experiencing the full beauty of PURE LOVE only happens WHEN YOU GIVE IT. When you become a wellspring of PURE LOVE flowing from you consistently, then you have experienced THE MOST BEAUTIFUL PART OF LIFE...And when the UNFAIR part of life hits you, you hit back by pouring out more love.

Leave no room in your heart for condemnation, malice, hatred, or prejudice. Clear all that junk out of your heart to make room for PURE LOVE. It cannot cohabitate with such things.

One of the great things about PURE LOVE is that it can be given despite your economic status, your level of worldly "success," or even your physical limitations...And by giving it, you rise above all those things.

Rise above the unfair part of life today and pour out some love. I promise you, there is somebody within reach who needs it.

My PURE LOVE forever to all of you who have supported me in so many ways ~

Tad Tomaseski

A Conclusion of Sorts…

So, once again, cancer rears its ugly head. We pray, hope for the best, and fear the worst. By the time you read this, Tad's medical situation will no doubt have changed many times over, hopefully for the better, but his prognosis does not appear optimistic.

Therefore, it seems appropriate to end this book with the uncertainty with which all my beloved oncology families have lived. Their fears, their tears, and their anguish in no way diminished their courage and indomitable spirits.

As for the children and teens I had the privilege of knowing, their spirits will live within me forever. Every time I look to the heavens, I will remember my special angels.

Epilogue

What do I miss about St. Louis Children's Hospital? Although I love Florida and never regret the move, there is a lot I miss about those special years:

…I miss seeing the kids in clinic every day. I miss their smiles, their spunk, their stories, and their hugs.

…I miss our great clinic volunteers coming into my office for that special toy or lunch treat, anything that would make life more comfortable for the children, teens, and families they were caring for.

…I miss talking to the parents and grandparents as well as their openness, honesty, and insight. They and the teens are the ones who gave me my real education on pediatric oncology.

…I miss the humor and brutal honesty of the teens. I especially miss working with teen patients who turned into my best volunteers such as Eddie, Todd, Shawn, John, and Goldie. I am sure they all remembered the golden rule of planning an event: use a pencil because you have to be flexible over and over again!

…I miss the support groups where laughter shared was twice as sweet and tears that fell were shared with understanding hearts.

…I miss being an integral part of such a committed oncology team that lunch was often a hastily grabbed cookie or handful of popcorn. I always recommended that new clinics be carpeted with white flecks to blend with the popcorn scattered across the floor!

…I miss the unexpected but very welcome visits by old families who mysteriously knew when we were low on prizes or birthday gifts and who came in with exactly what we needed. I always said our "angels" prompted them.

…I miss the young pediatric fellows coming into my office every evening looking for a cookie or piece of candy to hold them over until they got their much-delayed dinners.

…I miss volunteers Jim and Connie Miles of His Kids helping coordinate events and coming in with another cartload of "goodies" for the families, filling my office to the point that I could barely sit down.

…I miss running around looking for a candle or match for a birthday or "You're off Treatment!" celebration.

…I miss Marnie Hauff, who after the death of her son came back for twenty-three years to help the children and teens with educational issues.

…I miss Mr. Kuhns coming with his bag full of handmade cars and trucks, each one lovingly made for the kids in clinic.

…I even miss the late evening meetings with dedicated volunteers and staff working to make each program a little better each year.

…I miss all the crazy, wonderful, and exhausting events and programs we organized in our attempts to help kids forget for a few hours or a few days that they had cancer.

Acknowledgments

I have been recognized for my work with children who were in treatment for cancer and for my work with Prader-Willi syndrome (PWS). I'm humbly aware that we do not do good deeds in a vacuum and that I stand on the shoulders of many special people. In this book, I would like to give tribute to those who were there for me during those important ten years of working pediatric oncology at St. Louis Children's Hospital.

The families I worked with whose children had cancer were my guiding light. They taught me what it's like, how it feels, and how the system can be changed to be more helpful. They gave me a wealth of information and insight that can't be found in the finest of schools.

Their children were my spark of joy. No matter how tired or discouraged I felt, I couldn't help but smile and feel renewed vigor the minute I got off the elevator at the hospital and saw their animated faces or heard their delightful stories. The children who did well gave me hope for the future, and those who had to leave us gave me a strong sense that death is nothing to fear. How fortunate I was to have the opportunity to learn from these children. They had so much to teach us all about courage, resiliency, and making the best of each day.

The staff at the hospital gave me a sense of community. Together we worried, cried, and celebrated each child's birthday and new head of hair.

My volunteers inspired me. Some parents took time from their busy schedules to come back to help others when their child was off treatment, and some volunteers helped just because they cared. But my greatest source of inspiration were the parents whose children had died. I saw them rise from the ashes of despair to offer their love, compassion, and knowledge to help the next child…and the next…and the next. I knew they would walk through hot coals with me to make it better for the family that was hurting or the child who was dying.

The blossoms of my love were my own wonderful children who learned at an early age to make their own dinners and that there was always room at our house for one more. They kept me based in reality and in touch with the myriad of feelings—hope, love, fear, pride—that parents experience. In spite of the many school events I missed while they were growing up, they still managed to turn out well. They knew that no matter how many "children" I had in my life, our love and home could always be counted on.

I saved Al, my husband, for last because he has been my main source of strength and nurturance. Although I'm the one who authors all the articles and gets the awards, he is the one who spends late hours at the computer helping make my "inspiring" thoughts readable. Even though I was the one on the national board for Prader-Willi syndrome, he was the one who spent thousands of hours with me late at night and on weekends developing our state chapter, publishing the newsletter, and helping me with board projects.

During our years at SLCH, this mild-mannered engineer picked me up at the hospital at 6:00 p.m. night after night. Even though he was hungry and had a deadline on a project, I never had to explain why we had to do something right then. Likewise, he never complained when I asked him to put on his volunteer pin and visit a family, play games with a child, or help me set up for a support group.

Acknowledgments

Al was also my "main man" at camp and didn't hesitate to help in every way possible, including letting kids paint designs on his bald head. He learned with me that some things can't wait until tomorrow. I have seen him tenderly carry a child too weak to get into our van, hold hands with the family while praying around a child's bed, and clutch my hand as we walked into a funeral home, understanding without words my need for silence. When my back went out, he was the one who gave me a massage and listened to the events of the day. He never said, "I can't handle these tragic stories." Instead, when my tears dried up, his flowed for me. Al is in every way my finest companion. Like Jason Struble said of his mom, Al is the wind beneath my wings.

Special acknowledgement and thanks also go to Jeff Brewer, who gave me the initial advice and courage to publish this book, and my friend Pam Akins Levinson, who gave initial editing advice when the book was in its very rough draft stages. Closest to my heart is our daughter and son-in-law. Tracy and Jeff White sponsored the cost of publishing this book because they believe in the insight it offers, value the lives it honors, and want to pay tribute to their beloved son. May Adam and all the angels in this book be remembered forever.

About the Author

*J*analee Tomaseski-Heinemann lives with her husband, Al, in Sarasota, Florida. She is the mother of five children and five surviving grandchildren. Raising a stepson who has Prader-Willi syndrome (PWS), she has mainly (under the name of Janalee Heinemann) been recognized for her work and writings nationally and internationally with the syndrome. She is past president of the national organization, Prader-Willi Syndrome Association (USA), past executive director, and past vice president of the international organization, IPWSO. Janalee has her master's degree in social work from Washington University in St. Louis.

Janalee worked, laughed, and cried with over one hundred children who died from cancer and also many survivors during her ten years in pediatric oncology. She is the recipient of the American Cancer Society Service and Rehabilitation Award and the John Krey III Memorial Award. This is the book she promised herself, and all her angels in heaven, that she would write before she joins them.